PENGUIN ‌
'LOVE ME ‌

Michael Braun was born in New York City and spent the sixties and part of the seventies in London, where he wrote for the *Observer* and the *Sunday Times*. On moving to Los Angeles in the mid-1970s, he worked in many capacities in the movie industry. He now lives in New York, where he is producing a musical on Broadway.

MICHAEL BRAUN

———————

'LOVE ME DO!'

THE BEATLES' PROGRESS

PENGUIN BOOKS

PENGUIN BOOKS

Published by the Penguin Group
Penguin Books Ltd, 27 Wrights Lane, London W8 5TZ, England
Penguin Books USA Inc., 375 Hudson Street, New York, New York 10014, USA
Penguin Books Australia Ltd, Ringwood, Victoria, Australia
Penguin Books Canada Ltd, 10 Alcorn Avenue, Toronto, Ontario, Canada M4V 3B2
Penguin Books (NZ) Ltd, 182–190 Wairau Road, Auckland 10, New Zealand

Penguin Books Ltd, Registered Offices: Harmondsworth, Middlesex, England

First published in the USA 1964
First published in Great Britain in Penguin Books 1964
Reprinted in Penguin Books 1995
1 3 5 7 9 10 8 6 4 2

Printed in England by Clays Ltd, St Ives plc

Contents

For

Polly, Janet, Elaine, Lucy, Shirley,
Carol, Susan, Barbara, Kathy, Patsy,
Mildred, Sylvia, Rose, Judy, Georgia,
Jane, Penelope, Madelon, Caroline,
Julia, Debbie, Sally, Candida, Muriel,
Jean, Nina, Pat, Evelyn, Imelda,
Dolly, Sybille, Frances, Jessica, Ivy,
Rona, Fanny, Edna, Ruth, Diana,
Betty, Amy, Lois, Tessa, Daphne,
Myra, Edith, Valerie, Antonia, Joan,
Yvonne, Nancy, Dora, Angela,
Phyllis, Wendy, Rachel, Deirdre,
Linda, Charlotte, Vivien, Belinda,
Pamela, Emily, and Jennifer

who wanted to know

Foreword to the 1995 Reprint

Even skilled bibliographers have a formidable task keeping track of every book published about the Beatles. A complete library would contain more than 250 English editions to date, and countless more have been originated in other languages. Few contribute much to the common knowledge of the Beatles' lives and work.

'*Love Me Do!*': *The Beatles' Progress* is decidedly beyond this criticism. Although written early, in 1963–4, and so relating only the first part of the Beatles' remarkable story, it may even be the *best* book ever written about them. Certainly, for insight into the Beatles' personalities it is unparalleled, and for those seeking the full flavour of the period in which Beatlemania began, it is engrossing and, in my view, unsurpassed.

Braun spent three months in the company of the Beatles and those close to them, as they worked first the British provinces, then London, then Paris and then America, and in '*Love Me Do!*' he skilfully reports these merry goings-on in a manner that engages and then drives the reader quickly onward, wrapped up in the actions of the Beatles themselves, the staff working for them, the pack of journalists following them, the police protecting them and the fans chasing them.

'*Love Me Do!*' tells-it-like-it-was, without fear or favour, and certainly without dressing. Indeed, perhaps the most striking aspect of the book is its candour. It is well to remember that Michael Braun wrote '*Love Me Do!*' at a time when the media refused to take the Beatles seriously. Apart from Braun, no one had looked beyond the 'long hair' or the 'jelly babies' or the 'yeah, yeah, yeah' angles. While others mentioned that the Beatles drank Coke, Braun saw no reason to hide the fact that they also took it with Scotch.

In short, '*Love Me Do!*' showed that the Beatles were human, with opinions, intelligence, likes, dislikes, pleasures and frustrations just like anyone else. It revealed that their vocabulary could go beyond the 'crumbs' and 'crikey' of Billy Bunter – a fact, clearly, that came as quite a blow to those intent on portraying the Beatles as squeaky clean. No doubt fearful that its readers might discover this, the Beatles' monthly fan magazine failed to mention that '*Love Me Do!*' had been published, and the *New Musical Express*, in a short review in November 1964, commented that the book contained 'pungent, sometimes coarse dialogue *allegedly by them*' (my italics). A week later, the same paper ran a one-liner, reporting, almost with disbelief, 'Michael Braun's new book on the Beatles attributes this quote to John Lennon: "We hate Cliff Richard's records"' (The very idea!) And, emphasizing just how much of an impact '*Love Me Do!*' was making, there was yet another mention a couple of weeks further on: 'Quoted in Michael Braun's book, George Harrison using bad language.'

The *NME* called Braun's book 'an image killer' and openly wondered if the Beatles would like it (clearly expecting that they would not). I imagine that they probably were not bothered about it one way or the other, but, if anything, would at least have welcomed Braun's portrayal of them as real people. John Lennon remembered '*Love Me Do!*' during his infamous soul-baring interview with *Rolling Stone* in 1970 when, after dismissing the Beatles' authorized biography by Hunter Davies, he commented, '"*Love Me Do!*" was a better book. That was a true book. He wrote how we were, which was bastards. You can't be anything else in a situation of such pressure.'

Nowhere else is that pressure as brilliantly portrayed as it is in '*Love Me Do!*', and no other Beatles book has ever captured its moment so well. Unavailable for almost thirty years, this reissue is a most welcome one, and I for one believe that it would be a sin for Michael Braun's volume – which ought to be required reading for all students and historians of the twentieth century – to slip into obscurity again.

Mark Lewisohn (author of *The Complete Beatles Chronicle*)
Hertfordshire

Preface to the 1995 Reprint

Music, when soft voices die, vibrates in the memory . . .
Shelley

In the early autumn of 1963 I travelled to Sunderland, then a dank and grimy town on the North Sea. This was the England of the dark, satanic mills – I felt I had journeyed into the past. The night I arrived I met the Beatles and sensed that I had glimpsed the future.

It wasn't so much their music, which in any case was hard to hear because of the screaming fans. It wasn't even the audience's delirious reaction. After all, I came from the culture that had produced Elvis. It was afterwards, talking with and observing those then known as the Four Moptops or the Fab Four, that I began suspecting I was in the presence of a new kind of person.

They were working-class urban lads who, had they been American, would have liked Frankie Laine, Frankie Valli or Frankie Avalon. Instead they listened to and talked about Muddy Waters, Little Richard and Buddy Holly. They were also interested in Fellini, Kerouac and marijuana. In fact they resonated to everything that we have come to call Pop Culture.

During the next few months, as we toured up and down the country, they riffed and joked among themselves, sharpening the collective personae they would present to the world.

> *Paul:* 'Ask Ringo what kind of music he likes.'
> *Me:* 'Ringo, what kind of music do you like?'
> *Ringo:* 'I like all sorts of music – especially Shakespeare's.'

They were a tight little island unto themselves, these four – and that is what probably permitted them to survive that time when the whole planet seemed to revolve around their sun.

Certainly, not before or since have so many people incorporated into their lives not only a group of artists' work but also their spirit. Who would have thought, all those years ago, that we would be approaching the Millennium with their words on our lips, and their music ringing in our ears?

'Imagine', said John, and as usual he had the last word.

Michael Braun
New York City
November 1995

Introduction

For as long as anyone can remember, the weather has been the main topic of conversation in Britain, but last year it had some very unexpected competition. Just as the Profumo–Keeler–Ward balloon was fizzling out, everyone became aware of four young men from Liverpool. At first people just stared at their haircuts; a few even listened to their music. Then gradually, as autumn turned to winter, all that could be heard from John o' Groat's in the north, to Land's End in the south, was Beatles, Beatles, Beatles. The island that had bravely withstood invasion from the outside for nearly 1,000 years had been conquered from within.

Britain's teenagers had been the first to realize that Beatles weren't bugs. The purchase of pop records accounts for a good portion of the £1,000 million they are supposed to spend a year, and the Beatles' first record, 'Love Me Do', had entered the national pop charts and their second, 'Please, Please Me', had become number one. They made frequent appearances on several television shows which are devoted entirely to playing pop music and which command huge audiences.

They were also heavily featured in the newspapers that report on pop music and conduct the pop charts and are read largely by teenagers. One of the papers, the *New Musical Express*, claims to have a larger readership than any other musical paper in the world. While those old enough to vote still hadn't heard of the Beatles, 12,000 lined up all night for tickets to a concert, and 20,000 mobbed them at London Airport, delaying the departure of the Queen and the Prime Minister.

Then in October the government went through a week of crisis following the resignation of Harold Macmillan. As rumours and politicians swirled through London the Beatles were besieged by a mob of the faithful while they rehearsed at the Palladium. Reports differ as to the size of the crowd, but the story provided a respite from weightier affairs of state and during the next few days Britain's adults became aware that 'Beatles' was not a misprint.

As a result of the publicity over the storming of the Palladium, the Beatles were invited to appear at the Royal Variety Performance. The programme starred Marlene Dietrich and most of Britain's top entertainers. On the day of the show the Prince of Wales theatre in Picadilly Circus was blockaded by a horde of teenage girls screaming for the Beatles. Miss Dietrich had trouble entering the stage door, and when the Queen Mother accompanied by Princess Margaret and Lord Snowdon arrived they were greeted by shouts of 'We want the Beatles.'

On stage, the Beatles sang several songs to a respectful, though undemonstrative, adult audience. Before the last number, one of the group, John Lennon, stepped to the front of the stage. 'On this next number,' he said, 'I want you all to join in. Would those in the cheap seats clap their hands? The rest of you can rattle your jewellery.'

Afterwards, in the royal lounge, the Beatles were presented to the Queen Mother. She told them she had enjoyed the show and asked them where they would be performing next. At Slough, they told her. 'Ah,' she said with obvious delight, 'that's near us.' Beatlemania had received the royal imprimatur.

From then on there was no restraining the press. For the past several years Britain's national newspapers have been engaged in a fierce struggle to attract the younger generation of readers. The popular papers reprint the pop music charts and patriotically bemoan the fact that the top-selling records have always been made by Americans or by singers such as Cliff Richard and Billy Fury who have studied Elvis, Avalon, and Anka and mastered American accent and presentation.

At first, the Beatles also sounded American. There was something of the Everly Brothers' instrumentation plus the style and presentation of The Miracles and Little Richard. But this time the beat wasn't coming from Nashville or Harlem. As one fourteen-year-old girl told the *Observer*, 'You usually think of film stars, pop singers, and so forth as living in glamorous places, Hollywood and so on. But the Beatles aren't like that. It's *Liverpool* – where *Z-Cars* comes from.'

In short, four local lads with funny but acceptable haircuts; who sang funky but were clean, adorable, and cheeky – but not too cheeky; just perfect for British idols. The press took a brief look and a briefer listen and with a whoop of pure joy from their circulation departments gave birth to the 'Mersey Sound'.

Since most people in Britain read at least one of the many daily and Sunday newspapers that circulate from one end of the country to another, within a week everyone was talking about the Beatles. The popular papers vied with one another to run versions of headlines incorporating the words 'Beatles', or 'Yeah, Yeah, Yeah'; the serious Sundays ran long analyses (the *Observer* printed a picture of a guitar-shaped Cycladic fertility goddess from Amorgòs that it said 'dates the potency of the guitar as a sex symbol to about 4,800 years before the Beatle era'). Their shaggy haircuts became a cartoonist's standby.

As an American living in England I was curious to find out

what was happening in this country I had always thought of in terms of sonnets and thatched roofs. I was helped somewhat by the papers. On the one hand the *Daily Mirror*, which has the biggest circulation in the world, said:

YEAH! YEAH! YEAH!

You have to be a real sour square not to love the nutty, noisy, happy, handsome Beatles.

If they don't sweep your blues away – brother, you're a lost cause. *If they don't put a beat in your feet* – sister, you're not living.

How refreshing to see these rumbustious young Beatles take a middle-aged Royal Variety Performance by the scruff of their necks and have them beatling like teenagers.

Fact is that Beatle People are everywhere. From Wapping to Windsor. Aged seven to seventy. And it's plain to see why these four energetic, cheeky lads from Liverpool go down so big.

They're young, new. They're high spirited, cheerful. What a change from the self-pitying moaners crooning their love-lorn tunes from the tortured shallows of lukewarm hearts.

The Beatles are whacky. They wear their hair like a mop – but it's WASHED, it's super clean. So is their fresh young act. They don't have to rely on off-colour jokes about homos for their fun.

Youngsters like the Beatles – and Cliff Richard and the Shadows – are doing a good turn for show business – and the rest of us – with their new sounds, new looks.

GOOD LUCK, BEATLES!

The *Sunday Times* took a more analytical approach:

Sexual emancipation is a factor in the phenomenon, though at a superficial level this may not be so important. 'You don't have to be a genius', said a consultant in a London hospital, 'to see parallels between sexual excitement and the mounting crescendo of delighted screams through a stimulating number like "Twist and Shout", but, at the level it is presented and taken, I think it is the bubbly, uninhibited gaiety of the group that generates enthusiasm. There is none of

Presley's overt sexual attack, nor for that matter any of the "smoochy" adult sensuality of Sinatra.'

I had seen the Beatles perform; I had listened to their records. They were enjoyable but no more enjoyable than scores of other pop quartets that had flickered briefly into my consciousness. What was fascinating about the Beatles (at least to me) was the things they said:

'None of us has quite grasped what it is all about yet. It's washing over our heads like a huge tidal wave. But we're young. Youth is on our side. And it's youth that matters right now. I don't care about politics. JUST PEOPLE.'

Ringo Starr, 23, Drummer (Ambition: 'to be happy')

'I wouldn't do all this if I didn't like it. I wouldn't do anything I didn't want to, would I?'

George Harrison, 21, Lead Guitarist (Ambition: 'to design a guitar')

'Security is the only thing I want. Money to do nothing with, money to have in case you wanted to do something.'

Paul McCartney, 22, Bass Guitarist (Ambition: 'to be successful')

'People say we're loaded with money, but by comparison with those who are supposed to talk the Queen's English that's ridiculous. We're only earning. They've got capital behind them and they're earning on top of that. The more people you meet, the more you realize it's all a class thing.'

John Lennon, 23, Rhythm Guitarist (Ambition: 'to write a musical')

'Why do you wear all those rings on your fingers?'
'Because I can't get them through my nose.'

Ringo

'It's disturbing that people should go around blowing us up, but if an atom bomb should explode I'd say, "Oh, well." No point in saying anything else, is there? People are so crackers. I know the bomb is

ethically wrong, but I won't go around crying. I suppose I could do something like wearing those "Ban the Bomb" things, but it's something like religion that I don't think about; it doesn't fit in with my life.'
Paul

'I don't suppose I think much about the future. I don't really give a damn. Though now we've made it, it would be a pity to get bombed. It's selfish but I don't care too much about humanity – I'm an escapist. Everybody's always drumming on about the future but I'm not letting it interfere with my laughs if you see what I mean. Perhaps I worried more when I was working it out about God.'
John

'Don't for heaven's sake say we're the new youth, because that's a load of old rubbish.'
Paul

'Naturally, I'm part of my generation. I like the way people bring things out in the open. I'd hate it if when you spoke about sex everybody curled away.'
George

'Do you wear wigs?'
'If we do they must be the only ones with real dandruff.'
John

' At school we had a great hip English master and instead of keeping us to the drag stuff like Return of the Native, *he would let us read Tennessee Williams, and* Lady Chatterley's Lover, *and* "The Miller's Tale".'
Paul

'I get spasms of being intellectual. I read a bit about politics but I don't think I'd vote for anyone; no message from any of those phoney politicians is coming through to me.'
John

'We've always had laughs. Sometimes we find ourselves hysterical,

especially when we're tired. We laugh at soft remarks that the majority of people don't get.'
George

'The thing I'm afraid of is growing old. I hate that. You get old and you've missed it somehow. The old always resent the young and vice versa.'
John

'I'd like to end up sort of unforgettable.'
Ringo

'Ours is a today image.'
John

I decided to find out what he meant.

Cambridge

Dear Beatles,

I hope you'll receive this poem 'cos we wrote it specially for you. (We were supposed to be revising for school exams, really.) We've sent a copy to your fan club too.

The Saga of the Beatles

Once there was a boy, McCartney,
Who was very strong and hearty.
One day he met George at school,
A handsome lad from Liverpool.
Together these two came upon
Another lad, whose name was John . . .
Now four singles to their name
They're assured of lasting fame.
So Ringo, John, George, and Paul,
Liverpool lads, we love you all!

Lots of love,
Paul and Narky

The police on emergency duty outside the ABC Cinema in Cambridge were rapidly becoming agitated. Great swarms of duffle-coated adolescents kept rushing to the doors of the cinema to ask a question and then returned sighing to the queue that stretched for half a mile down Regent Street. A large number of the crowd did not have tickets for the show. What they were hoping for was a glimpse of the chief performers arriving at the theatre. They were disappointed. Four hours before the curtain was scheduled to rise the Cambridge Police had driven to a pre-arranged rendezvous a mile from town and the Beatles had arrived at the theatre in the back of a police van.

Inside the circle lobby of the cinema they were now meeting the press. This pre-show conference had become obligatory since the Palladium siege had made them Big News. Each of the four was surrounded by his own little cluster of reporters and photographers. On the walls large photos of players looked benignly down. On the table to the side, a bar had been set up that prominently featured Pepsi-Cola and a selection of whiskies.

'What will your film be about?' asks a reporter of the Beatle I recognized as Paul McCartney. 'Sort of a fantasy type thing?'

'Well, yeah,' replies Mr McCartney who is wearing, as are his three colleagues, a grey suit, with a white button-down shirt and a black tie. As he talks I notice that his features, which photograph so delicately, seem much harder in person.

In another corner John Lennon is sipping a coke which he keeps replenishing with Scotch.

'How long do you think the group will last?' somebody asks.

'About five years.'

'Will the group stay together?'

'Don't know,' says Mr Lennon and pours another Scotch into the coke.

On the side of the room Ringo Starr is huddled on a sofa talking with two girls from a woman's magazine. George Harrison is standing at the bar re-filling his glass.

The manager of the cinema walks over to the assistant manager, turns towards the bar, and pointing at George asks, 'Which one is he?'

Backstage at the ABC Cinema all the performers including the Beatles were crowded into one large dressing-room. A few of them play cards on upturned suitcases; others are tuning their guitars. Paul McCartney walks in and out among the groups.

'Is everybody having a good time?' he asks.

John Lennon in a black polo-necked sweater is walking around shouting, 'All visitors ashore, please, the ship is leaving. All ashore.'

Someone comes over and shows Lennon and McCartney a picture of them smiling.

'Lots of teeth in that picture,' says Paul.

'We like to get our teeth into things,' says John.

A few doors away in a tiny dressing-room Peter Yolland was setting up tape-recording equipment. Mr Yolland was directing the Beatles' Christmas Show which was to be presented at the Finsbury Park Astoria Cinema in London. Because of the screams that usually accompany a Beatle performance he had decided to pre-record their lines, and he was there that night for this purpose.

The sketch, which Mr Yolland said would be the comedy highlight of the show, was a satire on an old-fashioned melodrama. The heroine was played by George, who was thrown in front of a train by Sir Jasper (John) only to be saved by Fearless Paul, the signalman. Ringo was to remain mute and occasionally dispense some 'snow' to sustain the proper mood.

The Beatles were scheduled to go on stage in half an hour and Mr Yolland had only this one opportunity to record them.

He had provided them with scripts of the sketch, and he now stood behind them with a stopwatch as they went over their lines.

'Oh please, who will save me?' says George.

'I will,' says Paul.

'Who are you?' says George.

'I'm Fearless Paul, the signalman,' says Paul.

The recording took twenty minutes. While Yolland was playing it back, the Beatles joked among themselves and mentioned the fact that their new record, issued that week, had sold a million copies.

Afterwards, Yolland displayed copies of the sets for the Christmas Show. 'I'm changing the concept of the pantomime,' he explained. 'I consider this a splendid challenge.' He seemed very nervous.

The bar in the circle lobby had now been turned into an emergency first-aid station, and the reporters had been replaced by a dozen nurses who stationed themselves at the back of the auditorium. When the Beatles were announced the audience burst into screams that hardly diminished until they left the theatre.

'We'd like to sing a number from our LP,' says John above the screams, 'called . . .' but he is drowned in a fresh volley of shouting. He begins to sing, squinting in the light, jaw pushed forward, looking like someone saying 'I dare you to say that.'

The boys in the audience clap and the girls rise out of their seats and fling their arms in supplication to the stage. The aisles and the area in front of the stage are patrolled by stony-faced stewards, policemen, and nurses.

Paul, earnest and boyish, is singing. 'No I never heard it at all' – cries of 'Paul', 'Paul', from the audience – 'till there was you.'

Some girls are now waving handkerchiefs. Others are sitting in a foetal position: back arched, legs folded under, and hands alternately punching their thighs and covering their ears. Most of the boys just keep their hands over their ears.

A girl sitting in an aisle seat cries each time the lights go up and reaches for the stage. At the end she stands on her seat screaming and crying. As 'The Queen' is played she stops screaming, but the moment it finishes she starts again. She is dazed as the stewards lead her out to the music from *The Bridge on the River Kwai*. Willingly and limply she goes.

In Regent Street the screaming goes on.

'Aren't they fab?'

'I screamed the loudest when Paul and George shook their heads. I've never seen anything so fab in my life.'

'When they talk it makes you want to faint.'

'I don't know. I guess I like them, but really Cliff's better.'

Backstage, a group of mothers and daughters were standing in the corridor outside the dressing-room. They had won a contest and were here to collect their prize – the Beatles' autographs.

John and Paul emerge. One of the women, flustered, says, 'I'm her daughter.'

'These new drugs really do wonders,' says John.

Someone mentions another performer who they think is beginning to act pretentiously. John says that the most pretentious remark he ever heard was once in Paris when he and Paul were sitting in a café and the man at the next table said, 'I feel like a scabbard floating down the Seine.'

I mention that I have read an interview with a pop singer in which he was asked what he liked to do in his spare time. 'I like reading poetry,' he told the interviewer; 'I've just finished reading a book of Beethoven's poems.'

At that point a girl comes over to George who is now in the corridor.

'Did you get that comb I sent you?' she asks.

'Do have a ciggy,' says George to Paul.

From the back of the circle during the second show you could only see hair and teeth, but you could hear better than in the stalls.

'We'd like to play a track from our new LP,' says John and is drowned in screams.

'The only thing they'll need after they've finished here,' says a nurse at the emergency station, 'is a good ear syringe.'

Outside, Regent Street was swarming with girls wearing sweaters with 'The Beatles' written on them. Two Indian students passed by.

'What exactly is happening here?' asks one.

'I believe it is something called Beatles.'

Two students in academic robes:

'Filthy exhibitionists.'

'What can you expect?'

MEMO
THE BEATLES

As many of you know already, the Beatles will be staying at the hotel tonight. It will be appreciated that during their stay they will not wish to be disturbed. It is strictly forbidden therefore for any member of the staff to try to obtain their autographs or to invite any friends on to the premises during the evening or the following morning. Failure to comply with these instructions will result in instant dismissal.

William Bradford
From the staff bulletin board of the
University Arms Hotel, Cambridge

Immediately after the show the Beatles had been picked up at the stage door by a police car, driven three miles out of town, and then taken back to the University Arms where they were now eating dinner in their bedrooms.

Outside the hotel a girl was telling a policeman that she knew they were in there, and that she intended to keep her vigil all night. She tried, but at eleven o'clock it started to rain and she went home.

Inside, in front of a roaring fire in the lobby, sat Neil Aspinall, the Beatles' young road manager. He has known the Beatles for years, since they all went to school in Liverpool together, and they call him 'Nell'.

Two dons asked how the Beatles managed to have any private life, and Aspinall said that Paul had perfected such a good disguise that on a recent trip to Sweden when he asked George for his autograph he was told to go away.

Aspinall continued talking and told anyone who asked that the Beatles had gone to sleep. In point of fact, in protest against not being able to participate in Cambridge's nocturnal culture, the Beatles and several friends were gathered in a bedroom of the hotel watching films.

The next morning, there were two Cambridge policemen stationed at the door of the hotel, but several girls had managed to get in and were asking the doorman what time the Beatles would leave.

'Beatles?' says the doorman. 'Are they staying here?'

Eventually their car, an Austin Princess WYO 898 is driven up to the door, and the doorman can no longer deny their presence. Pointing to two brawny giants he tells the girls that they are more important than Beatles – 'They're international rugby players.'

At the reception desk the assistant manager is telling a guest that when the Beatles were in Cambridge several months previously 'You couldn't give tickets away.'

Elderly bellboy: 'Beatlemania, I think they call it.'

Doorman: 'I think it's Beatlechasing.'

A car starts to drive in and immediately the empty lobby is filled with several dozen secretaries and waitresses who appear as suddenly as a stage entrance and as quickly disappear when the rumour of their departure proves immature.

Upstairs, while the chief housekeeper hovers protectively, John oversleeps two and a half hours.

At noon they leave Cambridge. The staff of the hotel crowds along the driveway. A small boy runs up for an autograph, and the doorman pushes him away. Across the road people line the pavement and peer out of shop windows. It is almost a royal procession although nobody is waving flags. However, a young girl standing just outside the hotel says, as their car moves into the midday traffic of Regent Street, 'I've never seen them *alive* before.'

Surbiton

Dearest Ringo,

Last night I had a simply fabulous dream about you and me. As far as I can remember I ended up as your clothes designer! I got another letter yesterday from Ron, that bloke who lives in Wolverhampton where your van crashed. Your van is in his garage and he's going to be sent free tickets for your show in Cannock – so he says! Lucky bloke! He said that he didn't think that my letter to you, which he read, was nutty, because he is a Beatle fan too.

I wish your van would crash outside my house with you inside it. Not a bad crash of course, just big enough for you to get out and wait for it to be repaired!!

I had a beastly evening yesterday 'cos I went to play your new LP and found out that my darling brother had taken it to his friend's house. I was so mad I felt like breaking his only record – Lonny Donegan LP – but I decided not to just in time! Everyone says how great it must be to have an elder brother – but they just don't know what it's like!!

Please, please, please write to me, Ringo. I'm getting more and more depressed the longer you don't write.

Your ever-hopeful Beatle-loving wack,

Janet

P.S. *I love you.*

P.P.S. *Give my love to John, Paul, and George.*

P.P.P.S. *Won't be long before the new* Beatle Monthly *is out.*

P.P.P.P.S. I HATE DONALD DUCK!!! DOWN WITH DONALD DUCK!!

This last reference was to a line in a widely circulated publicity release which stated that while Ringo liked fast cars and Brigitte Bardot he didn't care for onions and Donald Duck.

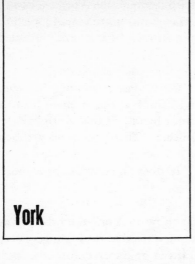

York

That evening in the dressing-room of the cinema at York two girls came in and asked to interview them. They said they wanted the interview so they could make a tape of it for a third girl who was ill in hospital. John sat in a corner away from the group. 'It's probably just an excuse to get into our dressing-room,' he says. 'Anyway women should be obscene and not heard.'

'Switch it on now,' says Paul conducting the interview for the bewildered girls. 'What's your name?' he asks Ringo. 'John', says Ringo. He then asks the girls their names. 'How did you like Germany when you were there?' asks the girl whose name is Eileen. 'We liked it fine,' says Paul. 'It was hard work,' says Ringo. 'Yeah', says George.

All during the interview they sign autograph books that had been sent to their dressing-room, and when they aren't actually answering a question they read letters from fans.

The girls walk over to John. 'How do you write the songs?' says the girl whose name is Daphne. John doesn't answer. Paul shouts across the room in a voice you use to an errant child, 'Tell us about the songs, John, tell us about the songs.'

'Sometimes we write them together', says John. 'Sometimes not. Some of them take four hours; some twenty minutes. Others have been known to take as long as three weeks.'

'What's your favourite song that you've written?'

'I think "Glad All Over",' says Paul, opening his eyes even wider. 'No, I'm kidding. I think at the moment it's our new record "I want to hold your hand". Is that all right?'

'Yes, that's fine,' says Eileen. 'Thank you very much indeed.'

'Oh dear,' says Daphne. 'It doesn't seem to have been recording. Sorry about that.'

Two hours before the first show in York the crowd was queueing beneath the theatre marquee that read 'Bingo every night (except Thursday)'. Fifteen minutes before the performance the doors were opened. In the lobby was a case lined with gold foil. On the foil were Beatle aprons and belts at 9s. 6d. The aprons were red and blue striped and were trimmed with a beetle playing a guitar and the words 'From me to You'. Decorating the case was a spray of plastic roses.

Inside, the compere is asking: 'Do you want to see John?' (Screams.) 'George?' (Screams.) 'Paul?' (Screams.) 'Ringo?' (Pandemonium.) They appear, and all during their act a man in a dinner jacket stands in front of the stage looking bewildered. The girls wave, hold up pictures, and scream. The man continues to look bewildered. After 'Twist and Shout' the screaming rises, then stops dead for 'The Queen'; but as soon as this dies out the screaming starts again.

Paul runs off stage shouting, 'Oh my God, my ulcer. Nell, do you have a ciggy?' Aspinall alternately hands him a cigarette and leads him toward the stage door where their car is waiting to take them to the hotel.

Immediately after the Austin comes a Jaguar driven by the

tour promoter, Arthur Howes. He is a short, intense man with a crew-cut. He is wearing a coat made of snakeskin. Two girls who work for *Boyfriend*, a teenage fan magazine, are also in the car. The photographer is a tall rangy girl called Fiona Adams, the reporter a redhead called Maureen Grady. Miss Grady is explaining to Howes why she doesn't take notes when interviewing the Beatles. 'It's really that I know them so well I know just what they're going to say anyway so I just try to listen to the way they say it.'

At the hotel, the two girls and Howes are joined by several other people at a table in the lobby where they are having a drink. 'I wish I was back in London,' says Howes, 'there's nothing more boring than an English hotel lounge; but I want the boys to know that I care; that I'm more than just someone who pays their wages.'

The Beatles are in their hotel bedrooms finishing their dinners. George feels tired and goes to sleep. John, wearing a T-shirt and an old pair of trousers, wanders down the hallway past the guard, into the room shared by Paul and Ringo. The table filled with the empty dinner dishes is at the foot of Ringo's bed. Ringo, dressed in pyjamas, is sitting up in bed. Paul, also in pyjamas, is talking about a film, *The Trial*, which he has just seen in London. He is describing a scene in which there is a misunderstanding about a word, when the telephone rings.

'Hello, helloho,' says Paul in a falsetto and then, realizing it is a friend, says Hello seriously. The radio on the bedside night table is playing 'Our Love Is Here to Stay'. Paul asks what days they have off the following week. Ringo starts to tell him, and John tries to confuse them by mentioning other days. The radio plays 'Old Devil Moon'. Paul continues to talk on the phone. 'That was "That Old Devil Moon" in a magnificent interpretation by the MacGuire Sisters,' says the radio. 'Now straight from the moon to the stars.' The radio plays 'Swinging on a Star'.

They start talking about their forthcoming appearance in America and decide they will not be successful. 'After all', says John, 'Cliff went there and he died. He was fourteenth on a bill with Frankie Avalon, and George said that *Summer Holiday* was second feature at a drive-in in St Louis.'

The radio played 'You'll Always Be Mine', and Paul returned from the telephone to announce 'We've been invited to a masque, what's that?' John tells him it means a masked ball. 'It sounds like a rave,' says Paul and returns to the phone.

'Wonderful singing by Mark Wynter,' says the radio. 'Only you would say that,' says Paul. 'Sure Trader Vic's is great . . . first the friends come, then the relatives of the friends . . . I mean the friends are bad enough.'

Paul finishes his telephone conversation and resumes talking about films. 'What I liked best in *The Trial*', he says, 'was when they walked quietly through the concentration camp. It was so dead quiet, just like another world and Elsa Martinelli in the background just necking like mad.'

'Now the Shadows sing to you', said the radio and I asked Paul whether he had seen *8½*. 'Oh, Peter told me to see that,' he said. 'But I don't know. I have this friend and every time he tells me to see something it turns out to be a drag for an evening's entertainment. He told me to go see *Next Time I'll Sing to You* and it was a dead bore. Then he suggested *A Severed Head* – it was the crappiest thing I'd seen for years. It's all this bit outside, "Well worth crossing the Atlantic for." Eccch, you can have it – crap.'

He turned to John. 'Stupid things like getting up in bed – no clothes on – fucking soft – they could have just had her herself without him getting into bed. I was getting bored and I spent most of the time watching this woman putting this scarf on and off and thinking that's not with it, tying it that way.'

He starts to joke with John and Ringo over just what is the right way to tie a scarf. After this he says, 'When I see an ordinary film – you know, one made without tricks – I know it sounds crap calling them tricks, but anyway, you get the idea . . . and then it cuts into a whole new action. When you're used to that it's hard to get used to the new kind like *The Trial* and *8½* I suppose. It sort of foxes me. I'm used to when they cut it's always a new thing happening.'

During the discussion about *A Severed Head* Ringo has turned the radio off. Now he turns it back on. 'Du-ah-du-ah. . . .'

'Uh, I need another drink, baby,' says John.

Paul goes to the phone. 'Hello? Yeah, send us six single Scotches – No, make it doubles, yeah, doubles.'

'Du-ah-du-ah . . . And now a number from Xavier Cugat,' says the radio.

'Uh, no, thank you,' says John, 'I always thought he was a kind of saint until I saw a photograph of his wife Abbie Lane. You know, St Francis Xavier with the cows.'

'No, he was somebody else,' says Paul. 'Assisi, with the cows or birds or something.'

The radio plays 'I'm in Love'.

John: 'Nothing better than British country and western.'

Paul: 'Ringo likes this.'

Ringo: 'What? I can't hear.'

Paul: 'Ringo has trouble with his ears.' (To Ringo): '*I say you love this song.*'

Ringo: 'I love the words.'

Paul (in heavy Liverpool accent): 'He loves the words. Have they brought your grapes then?'

Ringo: 'No, they didn't bother today.'

Paul: 'We brought you a couple of eggs.'

Ringo: 'Put them in here and the nurse will take them and do them for me.'

Paul: 'Have you got your potty?'

Ringo: 'It's in there in the bath-tub. You've changed your hair since you last came to see me.'

Paul: 'Well, keep a fresh mind about all things.'

There is a moment of silence. Then Paul says that people

from the Dingle in Liverpool have a basic fear of hospitals and always seem to bring people eggs.

'You see,' says John, 'psychologically they still regard the egg as something precious from the harder years. The egg is a sort of symbol of fertility and wealth.'

John notices that the radio has been turned off and asks who did it. Both Ringo and Paul deny it and John says he saw Ringo do it.

Paul: 'Tension is mounting.'

John: 'Tension all shipping.'

Paul: 'I once knew a fellow on the Dingle who had two dads. He used to call them number one dad and number two dad. Now apparently number one dad wasn't nice. He used to throw the boy on the fire – which can develop a lot of complexes in a young lad.'

Ringo: 'I remember my uncle putting the red-hot poker on me, and that's no lie. He was trying to frighten me.'

Paul: 'Tell me, Ringo, do all your relatives go around applying red hot pokers to you?'

John: 'It's the only way they can identify them.'

Paul: 'You see, Ringo comes from a depressed area.'

John: 'Some people call it the slums.'

Ringo: 'No, the slums are farther.'

The drinks arrive and they begin discussing the derivation of American names like Melvin, Clyde, and Dusty. They say that most of the slang that they have picked up is American Negro slang.

'Except that we get it late,' says John. 'For instance, we say "with it", which went out in America two years ago. And also, we sing "Yeah, Yeah", that went out a couple of years ago although it's still featured by American coloured groups.'

They start to talk about fads and how they get started. 'For instance,' says Paul, 'it's taken a long time for the papers to realize that we've caught on. We knew a year ago that we were catching on. But it's taken until this Command performance for the papers to say, "What is this thing?" I mean when Maureen Cleave wrote her first thing in the *Evening Standard* we thought it was just a piece of old hat.'

'The thing is,' says John, 'British journalists refused to accept that we were nothing more than ordinary in the pop world and they just weren't interested, you see.'

'A fella called Dick Fontaine from Granada TV in Manchester came to the Cavern to see us,' said Paul. 'He was raving. He kept saying, "I must do a film with you fellas." Nobody wanted to know. They actually made the film and of course they show it now.'

Another thing they say hurt them was being from Liverpool. Paul recalls that their manager Brian Epstein was told, 'You'll never make it, from the provinces. Move down to London and you'll really get moving.' 'Our publicity man had trouble getting things in the paper because as soon as people heard Liverpool they thought we were all from the docks with sideboards. And the name. Practically everybody who knew told us to change it. "Beatles?" they'd say. "What does that mean?" '

They talked about Dick Rowe, an A. and R. man at Decca Records who had turned them down when they first sent in demonstration tapes.

'He must be kicking himself now,' says Paul.

'I hope he kicks himself to death,' says John.

'I don't blame him for turning us down,' says Paul.

They started discussing the feelings of adults towards pop music. 'We're definitely fighting a prejudice,' says John.

'That's why I'm interested in John getting his book out,' says Paul. 'I mean, I haven't got a cut or anything. It's just that one of us would be doing something to make people notice. I mean, it's the same as if one of us wrote a musical. People would get rid of their prejudice and stop thinking that pop people can only sing or go into a dance routine.'

'Which is what the normal pop artist does,' says John. 'He learns to tap-dance. We don't want to learn to dance or take elocution lessons.'

'People keep asking us whether we're going to broaden our scope,' says Paul. 'I don't know whether we will or not. One of the things about us is that we intrigue people. We seem a little bit different. If you read about Cliff Richard you know the things that he says; you've read about them before. But us . . . it's like when Maureen Cleave interviewed us – she asked us what we were doing culturally. I had read about *The Representative* and said I wanted to see it. She was reading *The Naked Lunch* and I said I was reading *The Packed Lunch* by Greedy Blighter. It's also like when people ask why they like the Beatles. Quite a few people mention the word genuine. . .'

'Which we're not,' interrupted John.

'. . . because they feel that's the impression we give. I remember thinking, about two years ago, "What have the people who have made it – I mean really made it – got?" It seems it's a sort of awareness of what's going on. I mean, I can imagine Sinatra to be, you know, not thick. I also thought, "What about the people who made it and then just sort of went?" I mean, look at Marty Wilde. I remember seeing him and being very impressed. Then when he started falling off I wondered what happened? Then we met him; and then we understood.'

They started to talk about idols and whether they have to have sex appeal. John said that Bill Hayley was the first person to sing rock 'n' roll but that he was too old to appeal to the girls that Elvis appealed to. 'After all,' said Paul, 'a young girl just couldn't see herself married to Bill Hayley.'

John said that they have been told that girls masturbate when they are on stage.

'We're still at the masturbating stage ourselves,' interrupted Paul. 'You just can't get any on stage. I'm joking, of course. Seriously, anybody that gets as much publicity as we are and who are idols, I hate saying that because we don't feel like idols particularly but obviously we must be by now . . .'

John starts to laugh, and Paul protests.

'No, I really don't feel like one . . . I really don't . . . that is

I don't feel like I imagine an idol is supposed to feel; however, anybody who gets this amount of publicity is in ordinary people's eyes a fantastic being; he always was in my eyes, anyway – y'know, Presley ... Well, anyway, today this woman came up to the car; she'd never go up to just anybody in the street and kiss them; I mean, she was about forty; she was just sort of talking to me and she suddenly grabbed hold of me and kissed me. I mean, I was definitely embarrassed. What is it that with anybody who has had this amount of publicity ...? It creates some sort of reaction which doesn't have to do with sex or anything. They just say, "Look, there's that person we've been reading about in our good-as-the-Bible *Daily Express* every day." It's like the royal family. You have to like them because you've read so much about them.'

'Why?' says John. 'I didn't like *them* even when I was little. I disliked having to stand, which sometimes I didn't.'

'Another thing,' says Paul, 'we get letters saying, "You probably won't get this letter; it probably will never reach you", and before they have started out on the letter they're sure it will never reach you anyway. Letters that start out, "If you read this letter please read it to the end". I mean, there's no hope of us reading it as far as they're concerned.'

'Then there's people like my cousin Stanley,' says John, 'who I admired as a boy because he had a car and a Meccano set; and, uh, now that I have, uh, made it he treats me as if I was royalty or something. It unnerves me; I mean, he's thirty and I'm young and it's, uh, rather embarrassing from my boyhood hero.'

'But maybe it's only human,' says Paul. 'I mean, I know that if one of us had gone up and shaken Cliff's hand only two years ago we would have leapt home to the fellas – "I've met him! I've met him, there you go!" – and we would have been like that ...'

John: 'Even though we never bought any of his records.'

Paul says, 'I remember the first time we did meet him. We were in the business and Cliff and the Shadows invited us to this great kind of party. I mean all I could say was "Oh, wait till I tell the girls back home." Mind you, I knew it was a soft thing to say . . .'

'Yeah, you're supposed to make up things like, uh, "What a great job you're doing in the industry",' said John.

Paul: 'Because we've never been fans of Cliff's.'

John: 'We've always *hated* him. He was everything we hated in pop. But when we met him we didn't mind him at all. He was very nice. Now when people ask us if he's a bit soft we say no. We still hate his records but he's really very nice.'

'I really don't think there is anything sad about idol-worshipping,' says Paul. 'I mean it's the same as when you haven't got religion, you can say "Isn't it sad that all the Catholics believe that there's a God and they go to mass every morning and get up early and those poor buggers have the priest as their god. I used to think they're having a rough time, until you think about it again and think they're the blokes who're having a great time, 'cause in actual fact they believe.

'I mean, we think a lot of people lead dull lives but they don't really. Like the woman who comes to clean our house and make meals. If I actually analysed it, all she does is get up in the morning, see her sons off to work, comes to our house, does the meals for us, goes home, watches telly and goes to bed and the same next day. Compared to us it's dull but for her it's not dull. She comes to our house, y'know, the great stars' house . . .'

John: 'You're a great star, eh?'

Paul: 'Huh? Oh, yeah, yeah . . . this is all purely fictional . . .'

John: 'What it is is that people will go to see the original instead of a copy. Like I took a look at the original mouldy Mona Lisa in Paris – eccch, crap!'

Paul: 'I mean, it's like the Eddie Cochrane show. We all used to think he was fantastic. I remember thinking before the show that I was actually there. I mean, it's the same thing as when you go to people's houses, mates, or people you used to know, sort of thing . . .'

John: 'Notice he said *used* to?'

Paul: 'And they have all your records – there's always one of them who will say "Give us a song". They want to see you, even though it will sound terrible. It's like why people want to see the film of Picasso drawing . . .'

John: 'Uh, he saw it at school. Uh, we all did.'

Paul (laughing): 'You see the film of Picasso actually creating . . .'

We started to talk about the reaction of fans. Paul said he thought that a lot of the reaction now came from what people believed they ought to do. I mentioned reading about the violent reception in Liverpool of *Rock Around the Clock*.

'I went to see it,' said John, 'and I was most surprised. Nobody was screaming and nobody was dancing. I mean, I had read that everybody danced in the aisles. It must have all been done before I went. I was all set to tear up the seats too but nobody joined in.'

'I know if I went to see our show,' said Paul, 'I wouldn't scream no matter how great I thought it was. I remember seeing the Eddie Cochrane show and there was this coloured fellow. Well, he walked to the front of the stage and did one of those great big actions, y'know, and everyone just laughed at him.'

We got on to the subject of the importance of fans and the press. Paul said there were so many people who claimed to have 'made' the Beatles in a short year that 'I sometimes wonder just who actually did make us.'

'You remember after that big spate of publicity we got in the national papers,' says John, 'which was uncalled for by our office. We were news at the time, and it only just happened we clicked in fourteen editors' minds at the same time. One day Paul was ill and I believe one of the papers wanted a picture of him. Nell told them they couldn't have it, and the photographer said: "You mean, after all the publicity we gave them – we *made* them." I'd like to meet this fella who said it.'

Paul explained that they never talk to the teenage magazines. 'They just make it up. I think they prefer it that way. Also photographers . . . We work much harder with someone like Robert Freeman or Parkinson than with the nationals who only want a cheesy grin. Of course, you have to start somewhere. What happens is that you get magazines like *Boyfriend* or *Valentine* first, then the *New Record* and *Show Mirror*. They will do an article even if you're not known. Then you get to the *New Musical Express,* and *Melody Maker,* which, though it's not the top-selling one, has a jazz influence, and you can talk sense to them. Then you really have to be very well known to be in *Time* or the *Observer* or the *Sunday Times*. I mean, the *Sunday Times* – a lot of the old codgers who read that just never know what's happening.

'But really your tastes change in everything. I remember when we first got a photographer in Britain. We got this fella Dezo Hoffmann. It sounded good – Dezo Hoffmann – when he came to the studio we did all our good poses. He's all right for a pop photographer. But I remember at the beginning of this year we thought Dezo was the greatest photographer in the world.'

I mentioned Avedon and Cartier-Bresson. They had never heard of either.

'What makes Cartier-Bresson so great?' asked Paul.

We talked about him for a moment and then Paul said that Parkinson was doing a book on the Beatles. 'As far as photos are concerned and techniques of photography it may all be very good. Some of the things looked a bit contrived. For instance he had over-exposed film and film that was so obviously wrong that they *had* to be great.'

'Uh, Robert Freeman thinks it's old, out-dated,' says John, 'but I suppose some think a lot of the things Robert Freeman does are out-dated also.'

'Parkinson's big thing with us,' said Paul, 'was "Where

did you get those eyes?" and he kept lining us up and instead of pulling faces we had to pull eyes. Uh, John and George didn't oblige. Listen, do you think this boy Avedon will do things for us? Because we'll hire him.'

'Right now we're using Freeman. He's sort of in-betweensville,' said John.

We talked about Liverpool. Paul said, 'There is a certain awareness about some people in Liverpool. Like Ringo; he's never been to school except two days. Three times they told his mum he was going to die.'

'Anyway,' said John, looking at Ringo, 'to be so aware with so little education is rather unnerving to someone who's been to school since he was fucking two onwards.'

Ringo looked up and said, 'My grandad used to ask whether my hair was too long for butting because he'd do it if I gave him any cheek.'

'Butting is a Liverpool term for hitting with your head,' said Paul. 'I remember a little hooligan boy saying to my brother, "If you don't watch out I'll butt you", which he did.'

'Butting,' said John, 'is the first move used by the Liverpool lout. I only tried it once but my opponent moved and I nearly cracked my head open.'

I said that sometimes a poor childhood was fortunate, that it could be a real handicap to have a famous father.

'Uh, I don't agree,' said John. 'I could have stood a famous father rather more than the ignoble Alf, actually.'

Paul said, 'I think it would have been a drag if my father was famous.'

'I would have enjoyed the money,' said John. 'Never mind the fame. I think it is a working-class fallacy that you have to fight your way up. I think there must be people who have enjoyed a happy and fruitful life without having to fight for it. People who are made great are only made great by people of the class they leave. Let's say there are five people from the working class and one makes it. He's only great in the eyes of the other four.'

Paul said, 'Frank Sinatra didn't have wealthy parents but he's recognized by rich people.'

On the subject of children they agreed that they would probably make the same mistakes with theirs as their parents did with them. 'I know when my kid is about sixteen,' said John, 'and I say, "Come in at such and such a time" and he does, I'll be saying, "At my age when I was told to come in I didn't." I'll say, "When they told me not to have sex I did; when they told me not to smoke I smoked." If he turns out to be one of them who does everything he's told, I'll be dead choked.'

'I mean, what's wrong with us?' says Paul. 'Our parents used all the old clichés and look how we turned out.'

John asked Ringo, 'Why don't you ever say anything except "I'm the drummer?"'

'I don't like talking,' says Ringo. 'It's how I'm built. Some people gab all day and some people play it smogo. I don't mind talking or smiling, it's just I don't do it very much. I haven't got a smiling face or a talking mouth.'

Paul (whispering): 'Shakespeare's songs – you like Shakespeare's songs – go on' (to me) 'ask him what kind of music he likes.'

I asked him what kind of music he liked.

'I like real blues.' (They laugh.)

'And what kind of poetry?'

'Mozart's poetry.'

'One more ciggy,' says John, 'and I'm gonna hit the sack; "hit the sack" being an American thing we got off Gary Coople as he struggled along with a clock in *Hi, Goons*. But I really never liked "sack", it's, uh, something you put potatoes in over here.'

'The whole thought of hitting the sack,' says Paul, 'it's so – so dirty, and it can mean a lot of things.'

'You can sack Rome,' says John, 'or you can sack cloth – or you can sacrilege, or saxophone, if you like, or saccharine.'

'Or sacrifice,' says Ringo.

On Tour

Psychologists have been trying to discover why the Beatles send teen-age girls into hysterics. One of them came up with this explanation:

'This is one way of flinging off childhood restrictions and letting themselves go.

'The fact that tens of thousands of others are shrieking along with her at the same time makes a girl feel she is living life to the full with people of her own age.

'This emotional outlook is very necessary at her age. It is also innocent and harmless. It is a safety valve.

'They are also subconsciously preparing for motherhood. Their frenzied screams are a rehearsal for that moment. Even the jelly-babies are symbolic.'

News of the World

The Beatles have been on a tour of one-night stands for almost six weeks. They arrive in a new town at about four in the afternoon and are rushed under cover to the dressing-room of the theatre, where they remain until the show. After the curtain goes down they rush out of the stage door and are driven to their hotel. Since most English hotels outside the large cities stop serving dinner at nine o'clock, the Beatles' evening meal has more than once consisted of cornflakes eaten in their hotel bedroom. The next day they are up around noon and the routine begins again.

The Beatles were in Lincoln. After the press conference Ringo developed a severe ear-ache. A woman doctor was summoned, and it took her twenty minutes to talk her way through the suspicious guards. In the midst of her examination Aspinall came in and asked her just what she thought she was doing there, then hastily apologized.

It was finally decided to bring Ringo to the hospital before the show. Dressed in an oversized coat, a hat pulled over his eyes, and glasses, he looked like Brecht being smuggled out of Germany. As he left the theatre a photographer took his picture.

At the hospital the doctor starts to examine him. The assistant area manager for ABC theatres is sitting on a bench outside the consultation room. 'He has to be on stage in fifteen minutes,' he says. 'Everybody's in a merry flap. You have to take charge. I like a drink and parties as much as the next fellow but there's a time for everything.'

The nurse comes out. 'It's a Beatles' occupational disease,' she explains, 'all that hair getting in their ears.'

Coming out, Ringo offers cigarettes to everyone. The doctor declines. 'He's a throat man,' explains the nurse. At the door the chief porter asks for an autograph and is warned not to say anything to the press.

At the cab a man walks over and announces: '*Daily Express*. Are you ill or did you come to see a friend?'

ABC man: 'He's come to see a friend.'

Express: 'What's wrong with him?'

Ringo: 'Don't know. He's still under observation.'

Returning to the theatre, he is greeted by shouts of 'Ringo', 'Ringo', and 'Operation Ringo's Ear' is over.

In their dressing-room the Beatles are shaking their heads like dogs after a swim, preparatory to going on stage. On Ringo's dressing-table is a fresh tube of Yardley's Shampoo for Men, to which someone has appended '– and Ringo'.

In the front of the house they are clearing the last stragglers from the first show.

'Search the toilets,' says the manager.

An assistant goes into the Men's Room.

'No, you sod, I mean the Ladies!'

In the manager's office beneath citations for 'Good Management and Public Relations' two assistant managers are talking.

'I'd make a pot if I was doing the booking,' says one.

'They wanted them to leave by helicopter in Nottingham but I said where would you land? On top of those old theatres?'

'The police are competing against one another to see who can get them out the quickest.'

After the show they were rushed, still wearing make-up, to police headquarters, to change clothes. As they were about to leave the police chief came over to their car, which was surrounded by about twenty policemen.

'I hope you don't mind,' he says, 'but my daughters will kill me if I don't get your autograph.'

They sign their autographs and as the car pulls away Paul rolls down the window, sticks his head out, and says, 'Ta, thank you, thank you very much.'

'Dirty sods,' says John.

They were to spend the night at a hotel on the outskirts of Doncaster. As they drove, the car kept lurching over to the right-hand side of the road.

'Uh, hey, driver,' says John, 'we're not on the Continent. This is England, where we drive on the left.'

For the next twenty minutes the car kept weaving on the road. John and Paul began to mumble prayers, and at one point Ringo began reciting the Lord's Prayer. Paul, sitting in the front, wrote 'Help!' in the frost on the window. Gradually the car came to a halt. The driver had forgotten to fill the tanks with petrol.

Aspinall climbed out and after a few minutes managed to hail a lorry. The four Beatles clambered into the cab with the surprised driver.

'As soon as we get to the hotel I'm ringing up Brian about this driver,' says George.

It was then 1.30 in the morning. By 10 a.m. the Beatles had a new driver.

A mixture of sounds is coming through the window of the dressing-room at Sunderland – the wind, as it slices off the Tyneside, and the screaming of hundreds of girls in the alley below.

In the room the Beatles are talking with a priest. Paul is asking him, 'Why are there so many big churches in countries where people are starving?' The priest doesn't answer.

Ringo pours himself a Scotch and Pepsi-Cola and offers one to everybody in the room. The priest takes one and George jokingly asks if he is allowed to drink. John quips about Aleister Crowley and black masses.

Paul starts to discuss the financial aspects of Catholicism. The priest says he is paid only a small salary. Paul replies that the Beatles are paid only 'the going show-business rates' and that if the priest wishes they can entertain at his church for nothing.

To convince them that money is really unimportant to him the priest tucks a ten-shilling note in Paul's pocket.

Aspinall sticks his head in the room and announces it is almost time to go on stage. The Beatles rush around getting dressed.

'I wish I had time to convince you fellows about the

benefits of religion,' says the priest. 'We'd have a real bang-
up fight. Naturally, I wouldn't say the same things to you boys
as I say to my parishioners.'

'Why?' say Paul and John simultaneously, as they run out
of the room.

The priest doesn't answer.

The Beatles managed their escape from the Sunderland
Theatre by rushing through the darkened auditorium to the
fire-house next door and sliding down a fire-pole. Then,
while engine number one clanged out as a decoy they rode off
in a police car.

At the hotel they gathered in John and George's bedroom
for a call from Australia. They were being recorded by a disc
jockey in Melbourne. As they talked to him several girls
standing beneath their window began throwing stones at the
glass. Paul walked over and told them to stop because they
were talking to Australia.

The stones stopped. When the call was finished they turned
the lights out and spent a few minutes looking at the girls
through a slit in the curtains before going to bed. The next
morning as the Beatles left Sunderland several girls were still
gathered in front of the hotel, huddling against the winds
blowing from the North Sea.

The De Montfort Hall in Leicester is set deep in a large
park. Around the perimeter is a high iron fence with many
gates. Tonight they are all with one exception locked. The
audience all file through this one gate.

The hall inside resembles a large meeting-room rather than
a theatre. There is no proscenium arch on the stage. The performance takes place on a large platform in front of flats
masking the pipes of a giant organ. Before the performance
begins, a girl in the front row, with 'Beatles' written in gold
on her red jacket, has to be forcibly held down by her friend in
the next seat.

Backstage, Paul is playing the piano with a sweater over his head. Ringo and George are putting on make-up, and John is ostentatiously removing the glasses he constantly wears off-stage. 'Mustn't spoil the image,' he says. They come on to the platform, and the screaming begins.

Paul announces the numbers and the girls sit with their hands clenching their faces as if they have just seen a vision. John makes threatening gestures to the audience with his fist. It brings more screams. 'In sweet fragrant meadows,' sings Paul, nodding his head angelically. 'With a love like that,' sing Paul and George, and a blonde woman starts to rush the stage. The policewomen in the aisles move in and lead her away. 'Twist and shout,' bawls John. 'C'mon, work it all out.' The sound is deafening. Hordes of jelly-babies are thrown on stage. Several autograph books, a doll, a shoe, and an umbrella wind up there also.

As they finish, a girl in a red sweater is reaching for the stage, shouting 'John, John'. 'The Queen' starts. She is comforted by her friend. As the anthem ends she walks out limply.

The house lights start to dim. On the littered stage is a plush doll with a note addressed to 'John Lennon – the most fabulous Beatle of them all':

Leicester

Dear John,

Although all the Beatles are 'fab' in every way and form, you are the 'fabbiest' of them all. I love you, John, so much that I bought you this cuddly toy, which is what I think of you as.

Perhaps you would give it to your baby. Please, John. *Will you write to me and say that you received it.* Please. *It would make just one girl so happy, if you wrote, it wouldn't take you long, although I would wait for ever. Because, as I've already said, you are 'fab'.*

All my love,

Susan XXXX

Backstage, the Leicester Chief of Police, moustache bristling, swagger-stick at the ready, is waiting for the departure he had been planning for weeks. As he mobilizes his forces, the rest of the entertainers board the coach they use on tour. As it pulls out of the driveway the crowds who have been waiting for the Beatles scream at the other performers who scream back. Any glory they have achieved has been reflected from their four colleagues, who are even now being shown out of town by the police.

Our correspondent does not get from Mr Epstein the impression of a brilliant manipulator, but of a shrewd young man who has caught the lightning.

Observer

Young television actress Jane Asher is the luckiest girl in the world. Because she is being constantly seen in the company of Beatle Paul McCartney. Jane met Paul while writing about popular music but says, 'He is just one of many nice boys I know.'

Daily Express

The north-west corner of the huge lobby of Grosvenor House in London was filled with clusters of people fidgeting. As an apple-cheeked young man carrying an Aquascutum package approached, several of them rose and surrounded him. A room clerk came over and handed him a sheaf of papers. 'Mr Epstein,' he said, 'the telephone just hasn't stopped ringing all day.'

Later, in his suite, Brian Epstein relaxes and pours himself a drink. He has just spoken with the last of the people who have waited in the lobby. She is a woman who has flown over from New York to try to get him to endorse a jewelled live beetle. 'They're rather fun,' he said, looking at one she has left, 'but it does seem rather strange, having to make money from insects.'

He explains that he first heard the Beatles while running his family's record business in Liverpool. Before that he was a student at the Royal Academy of Dramatic Art, but he says that when he heard them 'I knew they would be bigger than Elvis. I knew they would be the biggest theatrical attraction in the world.'

Epstein excuses himself to change his clothes and then suggests dinner. 'I've heard the Coq d'Or is amusing. Why don't we go there?' At the table he studies the wine list carefully and when he has finally decided on a dry white wine he leans back and recalls that his task with the Beatles at first was to let them retain their vitality, 'but make them dress more tidily'. He says he flogged their demonstration records for a year before anyone would listen. During the meal he talks about the other groups he is managing. He seems to be slightly hesitant about moving his office from Liverpool to London, 'but I guess it's inevitable'.

Over coffee he thinks for a while. 'Most managers are L.s.d. men,' he says finally. 'I guess I have to be one too but I'm not really one at heart. I'd much rather be out on the road with the boys, looking after them. My one dream is seeing the four boys in their dressing-room. No journalists, no fans, no theatre people – just the boys.'

Outside the Associated TeleVision studios at Elstree there was a crowd of girls carrying signs reading 'We want the Beatles'. Inside Studio C, the objects of their affections were rehearsing for an appearance on *The Morecambe and Wise Show*. They were appearing in a sketch, wearing striped blazers and straw hats. While they were singing 'Moonlight Bay', Eric Morecambe put on a Cardin jacket and a Beatle wig and accompanied them by shouting 'Yeah, Yeah, Yeah'. Morecambe asked them how it feels to be famous. 'Not like in your day,' said John. 'My father told me about you.' They continued rehearsing the sketch. 'If you don't get a laugh on short hairy heads,' said Wise, 'try saying . . .' He is interrupted by a tall blonde in a leopard coat who asks them to pose for some photographs.

They line up.

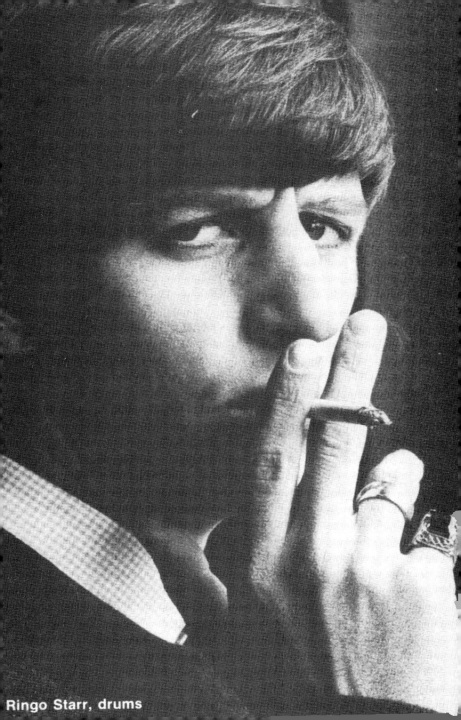

Ringo Starr, drums

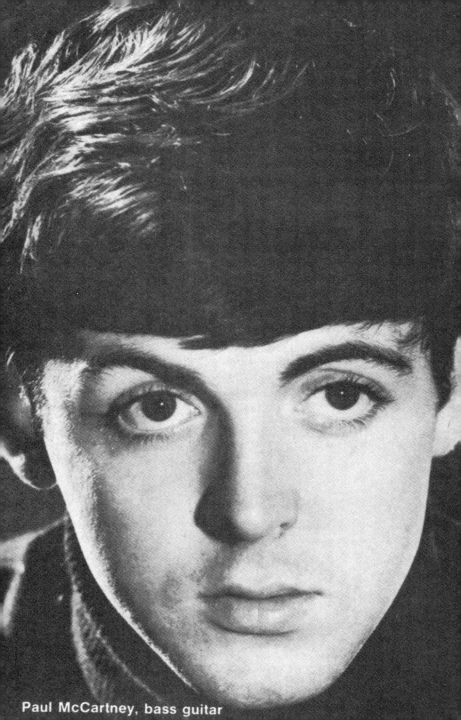

Paul McCartney, bass guitar

John Lennon, rhythm guitar

George Harrison, lead guitar

Pre-Ringo Beatles Group in Hamburg showing (left to right):

Pete Best   **George Harrison**

John Lennon   **Paul McCartney**   **Stuart Sutcliffe**

Brian Epstein, Beatles' manager

The Cavern, Liverpool

Recording Session

EMI A and R man, George Martin, with John Lennon

Pre-recording session

John Lennon

'Round the Beatles'

'Head up,' says Dezo Hoffmann. 'Paul, up the head.'

'Get a camera in there,' says a man from ATV. 'That's important.'

'George, could you look more interested?'

After a few minutes of posing in several groupings Wise says, 'Do you want us to fly?' and the photo session is over.

Sitting on the side observing were Epstein and a balding man with a county accent and a three-piece suit. He is Brian Sommerville, the Beatles' new personal-publicity man.

A few seats away the producer of the programme is telling a colleague, 'The show won't be aired for a couple of months. Let's hope they're still popular then.' His secretary asks Paul for his autograph. 'It's not for me, but my niece will kill me if I don't get it.'

After the show was taped, the chief writer accompanied by his two children visited Paul in his dressing-room. The Beatles were appearing in cabaret for the first time in a charity benefit at Grosvenor House, and Paul asked him for a line to introduce their act. 'We thought of something about being at the hotel and trying to get room service and then suddenly we were at this great big ball, but that sounded kind of soft.'

'You must get a laugh,' said the writer. 'If you start to announce and John starts to announce, so you're saying it together; then you stop and look at each other; then you both start again at the same time; then you look at each other and *then* Ringo from way up there announces the number – *Must* get a laugh!'

Noticing Paul's look the writer told him to think about the opening and thanked him for the autographs for his children.

That night in a suite in Grosvenor House they were still trying to think of an opening line. Someone suggested one based on the news in the evening papers. 'No,' said John, 'nothing topical, I just couldn't say it.'

Epstein recalled that at the Command performance he had

asked John how he would get that kind of audience to join in. 'I'll just ask them to rattle their fucking jewellery,' John had said, and with obvious deletions the statement had remained, and become the Beatles' most widely quoted line.

The Grand Ballroom of Grosvenor House was crowded with the elite of British show business. Girls in Diors sat at the edge of the dance floor. Whatever opening line the Beatles *did* use was drowned in the screams that greeted their appearance. During their first number the wires on their electric guitars got crossed and a drunk in a dinner jacket started heckling. 'Shuddupp,' said Paul, and the audience applauded. After their second encore they were rushed by a mob of people in gowns and dinner jackets. In an effort to get people to dance Cyril Stapleton led his orchestra into 'Twist and Shout'.

In the corridor Sommerville was frantic. 'I must get hold of a doctor,' he says. 'John is very sick but the press mustn't know.' When he gets to the suite he asks how John is. 'He's fine,' says Paul. 'We just said he was sick so we could get away from the mob.'

Sommerville looks at him querulously and asks, 'Did you see Dora Bryan?'

'Yeah,' says George, 'she put her hand on my shoulder and kept screaming "Twist and shout, twist and shout".'

Sommerville tells them that the chairman of the ball, the Countess of Westmorland, wants to see them.

'Tell her to piss off,' says John who is sitting on a sofa, looking glum. 'If anybody tells us we were good tonight I'll spit in their faces; we were awful.'

While John reflects on the performance, Paul goes into the hallway of the suite to talk with Lady Westmorland. Suddenly he comes running back to the sitting-room.

'Hey, c'mon and look,' he says. 'She's not an old hag at all . . . she's kinda cute.'

London

A few days later I visited John at his flat. His wife Cynthia sat with us round the fire, hardly talking, but occasionally getting up to look at their young son or to make tea. Toys that had been sent to the child lay scattered about. In a corner was a suitcase, holding John's stage outfits. Piles of records were on the gramophone and the Miracles and the Shirelles played during our conversation. John was wearing a T-shirt and the heavy horn-rimmed glasses he never uses on stage. He sat sprawled over a chair, looking relaxed, but he was still feeling depressed about their cabaret performance.

'The sound is so important and we just didn't have it at Grosvenor House,' he says. 'I remember when we made our first recording. We didn't sound natural. Paul sang "Till there was you", and he sounded like a woman. I sang "Money", and I sounded like a madman. By the time we made our demos of "Hello, Little Girl" and "Love of the Loved" we were okay, I think.'

I ask him whether he thinks the Beatles' success depends more on their sound or on the way they look. 'We could have managed, looking like we look,' he replies, 'and making worse records, or we could have managed, looking like the average pop singer and making our noise. But the combination makes a better impact. We have always looked different from the rest of the mob. We're clean-cut now but originally we were anti-clean-cut. I mean if we looked like Presley we'd look stupid. Before he came nobody here looked like him. But when we started there were already people like art students who looked like us.'

We talk about Presley whom John says he admires. 'Of course,' he says, 'he's doing the same thing in films that he did on stage but he's made a million and that's what he started out to do. I like him but I don't want to imitate him. Some of our songs are American but when we sang them American they just didn't come off. We learnt you just can't be American. When we first sang "From Me to You" it sounded American and we didn't want it.'

He starts to talk about the film the Beatles would be making. 'After this film,' he says, 'they'll find out we're not actors and that will be that. If we had a year to do it it might be good. But we're going to race through it and I'll probably lose all confidence by the time it's over unless something happens quick.

'I mean, none of us are going to learn our lines. I'm not, for a start. I just don't have the concentration. They're going to have to catch us and there's always one of us who will not, y'know, help.'

I suggest that maybe they could improvise their parts instead of learning lines. 'We're not really capable of ad-libbing,' says John, 'unless it's among ourselves, and that's too personal. I mean, I can count the people on my fingers who can understand what we're about all the time. No, the film will start out as one thing and I hope by the end that they will have gathered that we're going to do what we do.'

He takes a drink of Scotch and sprawls even more. 'Anyway,' he says, 'I hate the first one. Like I hated doing the first record. If we could only make this our first and fifth film.' He thinks for a moment. 'The trouble is,' he says, 'it's only us who can write for us.' He explains that his first line in the script is one he is supposed to say when Paul enters with an old man. 'I'm supposed to say, "Uh, who's your friend, Paul?" I wouldn't say that. I'd just say, "Who's the old crip?"'

Cynthia left the room for a moment. 'Uh, can I just go and get this thing I wrote and see how it affects you,' he says. He returns with a couple of pieces of hotel note-paper. On them, scrawled on both sides, was a story called 'No Flies on Frank'.

'There were no flies on Frank that morning,' it began. 'After all, why not? He was a responsible citizen with a wife and a child, wasn't he? It was a typical Frank morning and with an agility that defied description he leapt into the bathroom on to the scales. To his great harold he discovered he was twelve inches more tall-heavy!'

When I have finished reading he says that he has written thirteen or fourteen similar stories while on tour. 'When I have about fifteen more I'd like to get them published. Right now, I just like showing them to people. It knocks me out to see what different people laugh at. I mean, *I* laugh at it all and everybody laughs at something different. What it is, is really our humour on paper. I mean, mine, more than Paul's and George's. It's easy for me to write them. If people like them I can write them till I'm blue in the face.'

He wants to call the book *John Lennon in his Own Write*, a title suggested by Paul. I say that since he also plans to do sketches for the book it should be called *John Lennon in his Own Write and Draw*.

'Right-hand draw,' says John.

I tell him that parts of his writing are very much like *Ulysses*. He says he has never read Joyce and the only influence on his writing that he knows of is Lewis Carroll. 'I don't go in for much of those culture things, like Paul,' he says. 'Just drop a name and Paul will go; I'd rather stay at home when

I'm not working but Paul goes out to Harry Secombe and *Lovely War*. I suppose I *should* like those things, but I just don't.'

I ask him what he eventually wants to do – whether he wants to continue in show business.

'Well, first of all,' he says, 'we're not going to fizzle out in half a day. But afterwards I'm not going to change into a tap-dancing musical. I'll just develop what I'm doing at the moment, although whatever I say now I'll change my mind next week. I mean, we all know that bit about it won't be the same when you're twenty-five. I couldn't care less. This isn't show business. It's something else. This is different from any-thing that anybody imagines. You don't go on from this. You do this and then you finish.'

He starts talking with Cynthia about a series the *News of the World* is running on the Beatles. John is worried because he thinks there may be something about his father whom he hasn't seen since his mother died when he was fifteen. He was brought up by an aunt and hadn't heard from his father until the paper received a letter from someone who claimed to know him.

'I don't want to think about it,' says John. 'I don't feel as if I owe him anything. He never helped me. I got here by myself, and this is the longest I've ever done anything, except being at school, and that was false.'

George and Ringo share a flat in Mayfair. Although the building is kept spotless, the flat is filled with overflowing ashtrays and record jackets strewn over the floor. In one corner the hi-fi set blasts music continuously. This is punc-tuated by the ringing of the telephone. Their number is un-listed but when they pick up the phone they hear giggles or a sigh and the sound of the receiver being placed back down.

The Beatles have a few days free and Ringo has gone to Liverpool.

It is now midday and George has just woken up. He

wanders into the sitting-room where he is fitted for a suit by the Beatles' tailor, Dougie Kingman. He then gets dressed and prepares to go out for lunch. Once in the street he keeps looking around for fans and seems both annoyed and pleased when one of them finally asks him for his autograph in Park Lane.

At lunch he tells about a television programme the Beatles have appeared on. The host, a Liverpool comedian called Ken Dodd, had said he was thinking of becoming a pop singer and wanted a 'down-to-earth name'. George had suggested 'sod'.

After lunch he produces a copy of a contract the Beatles made in Germany. He is taking it to their music publisher to find out how much they are owed in royalties. He has been carrying it in his pocket for two weeks. Before that it lay in a suitcase in Liverpool and London for three years.

A few days later John is in a taxi, passing a store that has a red night-shirt in the window. He tells the cab to stop, goes inside, and asks how much the night-shirt costs. 'Six pounds,' he is told. 'That's a lot,' he says, 'but I think Cyn would like it.' While it is being wrapped the clerk asks him to look at some jackets that have just arrived. He winds up buying three and a coat. The bill comes to £107, but he doesn't have his cheque-book with him. The store presents a blank cheque but he can't remember what branch his account is at.

The next day the Beatles are an hour early for a recording at the BBC. Rather than return to their flats, George says he needs a shirt. They send Sommerville into Simpson's to announce their arrival and are then ushered into a room next to the executive offices, where, as a store executive informs them, 'The royal family does its shopping'. George gets his shirt and between them they spend several hundred pounds on clothes they cannot possibly get the chance to wear.

Dr Richard Asher is a physician who runs a psychiatric clinic at London's Middlesex Hospital. The study of his house in Welbeck Street is filled with paintings and books. Copies of scientific journals lie scattered about. Tonight, his daughter Jane is sitting in the study talking to a friend of her brother's, a young Cambridge student called John Dunbar.

Paul walks in. Jane says that since stories about them have appeared in the papers she has been receiving many telephone calls from girls who ask for Paul and then hang up. She says that her father must keep his number public because of his practice and that he is getting annoyed with the calls.

Her brother Peter comes in with his friend Gordon. They have just finished playing jazz at the Pickwick Club, and they start talking about a record they are about to make of a song written by Paul and John. Paul goes out, and I tell Peter about the Beatles' shopping expedition. He seems particularly interested in the fact that George spent so much money on clothes. Dunbar remarks that his only problem about clothes is that his parents don't like him to wear jeans all the time.

When Paul returns, Dunbar, who is reading psychology at Cambridge, starts talking about dreams and their interpretation. Paul tells about a recurring dream he has, with a discus thrower in it. Jane and Dunbar try to analyse it, but Paul seems content merely to relate it. Peter and Gordon leave to play chemmy in a Soho club, and Dunbar and Jane continue to talk about the interpretation of dreams. As they talk Paul suddenly stands up and announces, 'Well, I've had a very tiring day making lots of people happy. I'm going to bed.'

Liverpool

The Mersey Sound is the voice of 80,000 crumbling houses and 30,000 people on the dole.

Daily Worker

To those who say 'what was good enough for my father is good enough for me', modern methods will not commend themselves in art as well as in transportation or heating.

Catalogue of the John Moores Liverpool
Exhibition, Walker Art Gallery, Liverpool

George and Ringo had gone ahead by train, so when John and Paul arrived at London Airport to fly to Liverpool there was no advance word of their departure. Despite this, several hundred girls gave them a screaming send-off. They were accompanied on the journey by Brian Epstein's younger brother Clive who explained that he 'just took care of the family stores and let Brian have the glamour'.

During the flight they talked about their home town. Although that week they were number one and two (as well as having three other songs) on the national pop-music charts, in Liverpool they were number three. 'That's Liddypool for you,' said Paul. When they arrived at the airport they were met by a handful of girls who happened to be there. As they walked to their car a man approached Paul.

'Aren't you Paul McCartney?' he said.

'Yeah.'

'I'm Fred Hoger. I used to know you when you were a fat little kid at the Institute.'

The Beatles were home.

Above a small doorway that stands like a beacon in the murky gloom of Liverpool's Merseyside is a sign reading: 'The Cavern'. Beneath it is another: 'This is where the Beatles started'. Several inches away, scrawled in lipstick, is a third notice: 'I love the Beatles, especially George's hairy legs'.

The door is guarded by several bearded young men who seem to speak a language of their own invention. Once past them and down twenty steps you are assaulted by an amalgam of moisture and music so deafening that it seems to be part of the humidity. The lighting consists of several red bulbs placed casually about. In an inner room, couples in leather, suede, and fishnet are kissing, talking, and dancing.

When the music stops a disembodied voice blares: 'For your pleasure: your favourite and our favourite, the Mark IV.' The girls in the room – all of whom look fifteen – scream; the boys look bored. On a tiny stage at the front four young men are assembling three guitars and a set of drums. All are wearing Beatle haircuts. When they start playing you realize they are also singing (and very emphatically), but not one word is decipherable. During the number the audience stands or sits on wooden chairs, in rapt attention. At the end there is no applause.

During the second number, the volume of the microphone is turned up so much that now each indistinguishable phrase is punctuated by a screaming feedback. Each time they strum a guitar the sound slices through the air.

The ceiling of peeling bricks is about twenty inches from their heads, which probably accounts for the deafening vibration. At various times people have tried to paint the bricks, silver in one place, black in another, but now they are just allowed to peel.

In the front of the Cavern is a snack bar that sells hot dogs and cokes. One of the performers is standing there signing autographs. A rumour goes round that Ringo will be in the Cavern tonight, and many of those present decide to hang around to see him. A girl standing near the entrance holds up a photo of Paul. She kisses it and her friends scream.

As it gets later the music on stage stops and they switch to records exclusively. The kissing couples around the sides increase; when they play 'Till There Was You', you can distinguish the words. When the last number ends, several men rush around, yelling 'Coats, coats.' A few girls ask where Ringo is.

'He never came,' says one of the bearded men. 'C'mon now or you'll get chucked out, luv.'

The floor is littered with coke bottles and cigarette packets. Outside, in the deserted streets, several boys are packing musical equipment into a battered van. Some girls are asking them for autographs and lifts home. In the gloom another sign on the building next door stands out: 'This is it,' it reads, 'Liverpool'.

I was told that Ringo had gone to the Jacaranda, a coffee-bar that stayed open all night. I went there and listened to the Jamaican steel band and the people talking Spanish and Polish. I also talked with the owner, Beryl Williams, a Chinese woman, who showed me the murals of Merseyside in the basement. They had been painted by Stuart Sutcliffe who had played guitar with the Beatles until he died of leukaemia at the age of twenty-two. It was Sutcliffe who, in bed one night, had thought of the name for the group. They had been called the Quarrymen, after a local school, and also Johnny and the Moondogs. Buddy Holly and the Crickets were popular at the time and they wanted an animal name. Sutcliffe thought of Beetles, and John, unable to leave a word alone, changed it to Beatles.

There was no sign of Ringo, and Mrs Williams suggested I try the Blue Angel, a late-night club run by her husband.

Downstairs at the Blue Angel the more adult part of Liverpool's population was dancing to Lerner and Loewe. Upstairs at the bar were Tony Barrow, the press agent for Epstein's NEMS Enterprises Ltd; Ray McFall, the owner of the Cavern; and Bob Wooler, the Cavern's booker and disc jockey. They were talking about the fantastic number of beat groups that the success of the Beatles had spawned.

'The last I heard,' says McFall, 'there were more than 350 of them.' Wooler says there were groups called the Undertakers, and Jeannie and the Big Guys. 'There's also a gang of Beatle imitators such as the Grasshoppers, the Bugs, and so forth. My own particular favourite is the Animals.'

Two young men come over to Wooler and ask him to play a tape they have made, at the Cavern. 'We've become so successful,' says McFall, 'that I'm putting up a new stage. We're going to tear the old one up into little pieces and auction them off for five shillings apiece. The money will all go to charity, of course.'

Wooler returns to the conversation. He tries to explain the reason for Liverpool's dominance in the beat movement. 'I think it's a combination of the fact that this is a seaport and we get the sounds from America first and also that it is a city of gangs. After *Rock Around the Clock* played here, a lot of gang members formed groups. They had their own newspaper, the *Mersey Beat*, and their own clubs, like the Cavern. As jobs became scarce they devoted more and more time to following the beat scene. The noise may be deafening but it's better than having them in the streets with chains.'

Barrow talked about the Beatles' appearance the next day on *Juke Box Jury*. 'It's the first time they've ever had a complete group on,' he says. 'Sometimes we've had other NEMS people like Gerry [of Gerry and the Pacemakers] or Billy J. [Kramer] on, but never a whole group.'

'If you'll excuse me,' says Wooler, 'Brian built his own Nemesis. As he gets more and more artists they'll all start getting jealous of one another and there will be dissension.'

I asked if Ringo was going to turn up.

'Ringo?' says Ray. 'He's been and left, mate.'

David Jacobs, the host of *Juke Box Jury*, was trying to decide whether he should stay in Liverpool for the night or fly back to London. He was sitting in the front row of the stalls in the Empire Theatre waiting for the BBC technicians to set up for that evening's show. His producer, Neville Wortman, was telling someone that the Beatles are the only people they would consider doing a programme out of London for.

'David loves these boys,' said Wortman. 'I remember him at a cocktail party in London the first time they met. Suddenly David came bounding across the room, shouting, "I got them! I got them!" – their autographs, of course.'

A few rows back sat the Misses Bettina Rose and Freda Kelly, co-secretaries of the Beatles' fan club. They were to play hostess later in the afternoon to 2,500 members of the north of England section of the club. Right now they were talking to Ringo, who said he had spent the previous evening at home listening to records.

Half-way to the back Paul was talking to his former literature master who had brought his family to the rehearsal. He recalled writing an essay on American humour, including naming as his favourite book Thurber's *The Bodley Head*.

After a break for lunch they perform their show for the fan

club, many of whom remain for the telecast of *Juke Box Jury*. After waiting an hour an announcer comes on stage and asks the audience to practise screaming.

'Act normal,' he says. 'Scream when you're told to.'

Jacobs comes on. 'In my time,' he says, 'I've introduced people from Sinatra to Crosby, and all I can say is I am as excited as you are.'

This brings screams which increase as the Beatles make their entrance and take their seats at the jury table. The first record is Elvis Presley singing 'Kiss Me Quick'.

'As nice as Blackpool on a sunny day,' says Paul.

Next is Paul Anka's 'Did you have a Happy Birthday?'

George: 'Yes, I did, thank you.'

Paul: 'I don't like people with a crack in their voice.'

John: 'It's in his head.'

On the next record, a song by Billy Fury, George criticizes the guitar and John says he doesn't like 'gallop songs' but they agree it will be a hit.

The audience for *Juke Box Jury* is cleared and another brought in for a special BBC television show. An announcer comes out. 'Don't scream until the curtain goes up,' he tells the audience.

'Please, curtain, go up,' says a girl in the second row, clenching her fists. It does; and the Beatles give their third show of the day, with two more to go that evening.

Immediately after the taping of the second TV show the Beatles rushed over to the Odeon Cinema where they were to perform that evening. There, they crowded into a tiny dressing-room to watch the two television shows.

During the half-hour telecast John was seen on camera only twice. 'Somebody at the BBC is a Lennon-hater,' says Paul. Shots of Ringo pounding at the drums came through with no sound.

'We were talking to a man last night,' says Paul, 'and he

said, "I've never seen you do a performance yet, old chap. I'll definitely be looking in." What's he going to say when he sees this?'

They are still discussing the programme when Aspinall comes into the room and tells them to get ready for the first show of the evening.

'Another one!' mutters George. 'We'll soon be needing pills to keep going.'

Brian Epstein sat behind his kidney-shaped desk in the NEMS office in Liverpool. He was talking into his new telephone that relieves you of the necessity of using your hands. When he was finished he said he knew there was criticism of the television shows but the Beatles had been paid three times their usual fee for it. 'Besides,' he said, 'a BBC man told me last night that they were thinking of renaming it "the Beatles' Broadcasting Corporation".'

He said he was 'tired of London-type restaurants' and suggested we went to a little Chinese place he knew of. 'There's really no atmosphere at all, but they do marvellous things.'

In the restaurant he mentioned that the *Daily Express* wanted to take a photograph of the Beatles standing in front of five million records to represent their sales. 'I don't know how we can manage that,' he said. He said he was having trouble with people who were using the word 'Beatle' on their products. 'We have the copyright but they always try to get round it by showing a beetle or by using the word "Beetle".' He then talked about their impending trip to America. 'They're getting top billing on the Sullivan show,' he said, 'and that's important. We've also been mentioned in the *Insiders' Newsletter* and the *New Yorker*. I've also hired a man just to do publicity in the States.'

Several people came over to say hello. He said they were friends from his days at the Royal Academy of Dramatic Art. He thought for a moment. 'You know,' he said, 'the Beatles never know until twenty-four hours in advance what they will be doing next. In a way I'm sorry they've been so successful. John is a very unusual person. I got to know him well when we went on holiday in Spain last year.' There was a pause. 'Now,' he continued, 'I'm closest to George; at least he's interested in the business side of the work.' Another pause. 'It's just that I'm kept so busy managing their business affairs and I must share them with everybody.'

Year of the Beatles

1963 in Inghilterra l'anno della Keeler e dei Beatles.

Il Giorno, *Milan*

They came to the Wimbledon Palais as if to a shrine. It was the first meeting of the London-area fan club and from early in the morning a queue of girls stretched along the pavement, through the dance hall, and to the bar where the gods sat behind a protective counter: John squinting without his glasses (gods don't wear glasses), saying, 'Hi there'; Ringo, in a dark blue shirt, looking, as ever, slightly confused; George smiling, and Paul glowing and gently admonishing with a wave of his finger all those who got too enthusiastic. Then, after a few hundred girls had passed, one girl fainted, another burst out crying, and a third lifted her sweater and said 'Touch'. After that they were all whipped through to the exit, where they emerged sighing, kissing their hands, and looking ecstatic.

If the bar was an altar, the dance floor was totally pagan. A high iron gate had been erected in front of the stage. They were auctioning pictures of the Beatles, and the larger ones brought deafening screams.

Then the real thing is on stage, singing 'When the Saints go Marching In'. The young women of London stand on chairs and scream. Every time Paul looks in another direction twenty girls shout, 'Pole, Pole!' Others, hands over their ears, punctuate their screams with cries of 'Joewge, Joewge!' The prettier girls stand with their boyfriends and just listen to the music. The less fortunate continue to scream. Lourdes has come to SW19.

Several weeks before, they had to be smuggled into a besieged Birmingham theatre disguised as policemen. Now, three hours late for a television show, because of a snowstorm, they are met by only a hundred fans and the Birmingham journalists ask them if they are slipping.

On the drive back to London they listen to the Top Pops on Radio Luxembourg. 'And now,' says the radio, 'you've guessed it: The Beatles – "I Want to Hold Your Hand".'

'They wanted to know if we were slipping,' says George to their recording manager, George Martin, who is accompanying them, 'just because there were 400 fans outside instead of 1,000.'

Eight of the top twenty songs that week were Beatle numbers. 'They asked me if I was crackin' up,' says Paul. 'Crackin' up? They must be soft.' While he says this he flails his arms in a lunatic manner and over the radio Dora Bryan sings the week's number twelve song 'All I want for Christmas is a Beatle'.

The Beatles spent the last week of the year preparing for their show at Finsbury Park. One hundred thousand people had bought tickets before the first curtain rose. In celebration the London *Evening Standard* put out a special supplement headed: *1963 ... the year of the Beatles.*

64

Under their picture it said:

1963 has been their year. An examination of the heart of the nation at this moment would reveal the word B E A T L E *engraved upon it. . . .*

Under the heading, 'Why do we love them so much? Because . . . Because . . . Because . . .', columnist Angus McGill said that 'like well-bred children they are seen and not heard'. The paper's pop music writer, a usually acute young woman called Maureen Cleave, could only conclude, 'Everybody loves them because they look so happy.'

Scene: A literary party.
Woman: 'What do you think of *The Group*?'
Man: 'Which group?'

During the holiday season there was hardly a family in Britain that remained immune to the Beatles. Their LP 'With the Beatles', blared from a million gramophones. Stockings with pictures of the Beatles were filled with Beatle wigs and egg-cups; under the tree were countless Beatle T-shirts, dolls, nighties, and suits. Bedroom walls were covered with photo murals of the group, and, if that wasn't possible, young girls erected altars in the attic made of photographs. A ballet in London had music based on Lennon–McCartney songs, and thousands of young men took up the guitar. Beatle haircuts were ubiquitous, and one headmaster banned them because he said it made the boys look like morons. One boy, faced with an order to change his hair-style or leave school, left.

During the last days of the year the Beatles reached the status of a national institution. While the rest of the British press rested, exhausted from dancing in the streets for the past several months, *The Times* devoted an article to the Beatles, and not to their 'looks of happiness, my dear', but to their music:

What Songs the Beatles Sang . . .
From our Music Critic

The outstanding English composers of 1963 must seem to have been *John Lennon* and *Paul McCartney*, the talented young musicians from Liverpool whose songs have been sweeping the country since last Christmas, whether performed by their own group, the Beatles, or by the numerous other teams of English troubadours that they also supply with songs.

I am not concerned here with the social phenomenon of Beatlemania, which finds expression in handbags, balloons, and other articles bearing the likeness of the loved ones, or in the hysterical screaming of young girls whenever the Beatle Quartet performs in public, but with the musical phenomenon. For several decades, in fact since the decline of the music-hall, England has taken her popular songs from the United States, either directly or by mimicry. But the songs of Lennon and McCartney are distinctly indigenous in character, the most imaginative and inventive examples of a style that has been developing on Merseyside during the past few years. And there is a nice, rather flattering irony in the news that the Beatles have now become prime favourites in America, too.

The strength of the character in pop songs seems, and quite understandably, to be determined usually by the number of composers involved; when three or four people are required to make the original tunesmith's work publicly presentable, it is unlikely to retain much individuality or to wear very well. The virtue of the Beatles' repertory is that, apparently, they do it themselves; three of the four are composers; they are versatile instrumentalists, and they do borrow a song from another repertory; their treatment is idiosyncratic – as when Paul McCartney sings 'Till There Was You' from The Music Man, a cool, easy, tasteful version of this ballad, quite without artificial sentimentality.

Their noisy items are the ones that arouse teenagers' excitement. Glutinous crooning is generally out of fashion these days, and even a song about 'Misery' sounds fundamentally quite cheerful; the slow, sad song about 'That Boy', which figures prominently in Beatle programmes, is expressively unusual for its lugubrious music, but harmonically it is one of their most intriguing, with its chains of pandiatonic clusters, and the sentiment is acceptable because voiced cleanly and crisply. But harmonic interest is typical of their quicker songs too, and one gets the impression that they think simultaneously of harmony and melody, so firmly are the major tonic sevenths and ninths built into their tunes, and the flat submediant key switches, so natural is the Aeolian cadence at the end of 'Not a Second Time' (the chord progression which ends Mahler's Song of the Earth).

Those submediant switches from C major into A flat major, and to a lesser extent mediant ones (e.g. the octave ascent in the famous 'I Want to Hold Your Hand') are a trademark of Lennon–McCartney songs – they do not figure much in other pop repertories, or in the Beatles' arrangement of borrowed material – and show signs of becoming a mannerism. The other trademark of their compositions is a firm and purposeful bass line with a musical life of its own; how Lennon and McCartney divide their creative responsibilities I have yet to discover, but it is perhaps significant that Paul is the bass guitarist of the group. It may also be significant that George Harrison's song 'Don't Bother Me' is harmonically a good deal more primitive, although it is nicely enough presented.

I suppose it is the sheer loudness of the music that appeals to the Beatles' admirers (there is something to be heard even through the squeals), and many parents must have cursed the electric guitar's amplification this Christmas – how fresh and euphonious the ordinary guitars sound in the Beatles' version of 'Till There Was You' – but parents who are still managing to survive the decibels, and, after copious repetition over several months, still deriving some musical pleasure from the overhearing, do so because there is a good deal of variety – oh, so welcome in pop music – about what they sing.

The autocratic but not by any means ungrammatical attitude to tonality (closer to, say, Peter Maxwell Davies's carols in 'O Magnum Mysterium' than to Gershwin or Loewe or even Lionel Bart); the exhilarating and often quasi-instrumental vocal duetting, sometimes in scat or in falsetto, behind the melodic line; the melismas with altered vowels ('I saw her yesterday-ee-ay') which have not quite become mannered, and the discreet, sometimes subtle, varieties of instrumentation

67

— a suspicion of piano or organ, a few bars of mouth-organ obbligato, an excursion on the claves or maraccas; the translation of African Blues, of American western idioms (in 'Baby, It's you' the Magyar 8/8 metre too), into tough, sensitive Merseyside.

These are some of the qualities that make one wonder with interest what the Beatles, and particularly Lennon and McCartney, will do next, and if America will spoil them or hold on to them, and if their next record will wear as well as the others. They have brought a distinctive and exhilarating flavour into a genre of music that was in danger of ceasing to be music at all.

If this did not establish the Beatles as members of the cultural Establishment it was announced shortly afterwards that John Lennon was joining Ernest Hemingway and Ian Fleming as an author under the imprint of the publishers Jonathan Cape Ltd. The news was announced properly in the literary column of the *Sunday Times*, which printed two of his stories and one of his drawings and said that 'A stalwart body of critics and publishers judge this marvellous stuff. A rich plumcake of verbal cross-reference, sophisticated punning, and semi-poetic wisdom.' The announcement concluded: 'The voice is young, sceptical, and northern. And these extracts are fascinating, whatever you may think of them, as the natural unprocessed feelings of a man who is normally only heard in mass-produced form.'

In the first week of the New Year, their recording of 'I Want to Hold Your Hand' entered the American pop music charts at number eighty-three. To prepare for their trip to the States in a month's time, they went to the EMI studios to record an 'open-end interview'. This was a prolonged introduction to their record which would be sent to American disc jockeys. By means of a prepared form the disc jockey would ask questions that fitted the answers the Beatles were recording in London and thus gave the impression he was interviewing them himself. When they finished recording, a *Life* photographer took pictures for a cover of the magazine to coincide with their visit. After twenty minutes George said he had to be at the theatre early. The picture session was over.

In preparation for their forthcoming trip to Paris, the Beatles went to the London office of the French magazine *Paris Match,* which is located in the *Daily Express* building in Fleet Street. Their visit there was supposed to be secret and they entered the building through the supplies door. While they were having their picture taken in the *Match* studio, the door opened. In walked Robert Edwards, the editor of the *Daily Express,* Peter Baker, the associate editor, and Peter Evans, the *Express* show-business columnist. They were told that this was a special interview for the French magazine and not for the British press. 'Oh no,' said Edwards, 'I don't want anything for the paper. I just want a picture of myself with the Beatles to give to my children.'

'I think I'll invite them down for the weekend just to see what kind of fellas they are.'
Viscount Montgomery

Brian Epstein's personal assistant Barry Leonard quit his job 'because the strain of managing the Beatles is just too great'. In an article in the *Daily Express* Leonard told about his experiences with the Beatles. Among other things, he said Paul wanted to leave the group and was trying to lose his Liverpool accent.

As the Beatles gathered at the office of their accountant, Epstein mentioned the story to Paul. 'Barry says you are trying to lose your accent,' he said.

'Couldn't,' muttered John, as he examined a likeness of the Beatles fashioned in papier mâché.

A few days before they were to leave for Paris, one of the two national pop charts reported that the Beatles, recording of 'I Want to Hold Your Hand' had been ousted from the number one position it had held for nearly two months. It was replaced by a record called 'Glad All Over' that had been recorded by the Dave Clark Five, a group from Tottenham. In his first interview with a newspaper Clark told the *Evening Standard* that he had 'the proudest mum in the land', a phrase that hadn't seen print for several months.

It was falsely reported that they did not play their instruments on the record but had them dubbed by other musicians. Many people in the recording industry felt they were merely the forefront of a mass retaliation from the mammoth Grade talent organization, who, until the advent of Epstein's Liverpool groups, virtually controlled popular music in Britain. The sisters of Cliff Richard, a Grade client, formed a Dave Clark fan club, and Richard immediately issued a statement saying, 'I'm glad the girls have such good taste'. 'In any case,' said the Beatle supporters, 'everyone who wanted to buy "I Want to Hold Your Hand" has bought it. There's nobody left.' At the same time, in its second week on the American charts, it was now number forty-two.

These niceties did not concern the press. Ignoring the fact that the Beatles had now sold more records in Great Britain than any other artist in history, the *Daily Express* reported in a front page headline: TOTTENHAM SOUND HAS CRUSHED THE BEATLES.

The cartoonists had a field day: in the *Evening Standard,* Vicky pictured the Cabinet in Beatle haircuts and the Prime Minister saying to them, 'How can I say you're with it, with old-fashioned haircuts like that?'

Cruellest of all was an Emwood cartoon in the *Daily Mail*: standing outside a theatre where the Dave Clark Five are performing, a group of young girls are pointing at a girl of about sixteen. 'She really must be old,' they are saying; 'she remembers the Beatles.'

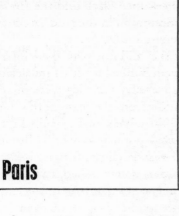

Paris

Several thousand girls were at London Airport to see the Beatles off to Paris. There were only three of them, Ringo having been delayed by fog in Liverpool. A half-hour after the Beatles departure, Maria Callas arrived from Paris to make her long-awaited return to opera in *Tosca* at Covent Garden. By the time Madame Callas's plane landed the girls had left the airport.

At Le Bourget they were met by a crowd of fifty French

teenagers and nearly a hundred journalists. They were followed into the city by hordes of photographers on motor bikes. The lobby of their hotel, the George V, was filled with more photographers. It was, said the George V's barman, who had been through it all many times, the biggest crowd he had ever seen, even for Brigitte.

The first night, John and Paul stayed in their suite, listening to records and reading fan mail. George, who had been signed for £100 a day by the *Daily Express* to write of his experiences in Paris, went to a night club in the Place Pigalle. His column was dictated to Derek Taylor, an *Express* reporter given to Italianate suits and talking out of the side of his mouth. The next day in his column George reported:

There are hundreds of marvellous chicks here – neat, very much in control of themselves. (I'm still looking for a Brigitte Bardot – the wild reckless type.)

If you look at a French girl she looks straight back and smiles. It simply means 'Thank you'.

Otherwise a smart French girl is very much like a smart girl the world over.

I think girls are here to stay.

All of the Beatles, apparently, shared a desire to meet Mlle Bardot. The following morning a large box of candy arrived in their suite. Accompanying it was the card of the director of their French record company. 'Unfortunately,' it read, 'Brigitte Bardot is detained in Brazil. Let's hope that these sweets will make up for her.'

The fog had lifted, and Ringo was on his way to Paris, stopping just long enough at London Airport to change planes and enable British European Airlines to pose him next to the 'BEA' of one of their planes, holding a sign reading 'TLES'. The cartoonists were also making the most of the occasion. Osbert Lancaster in the *Daily Express* showed a statue of Napoleon with a Beatle haircut and Illingworth in the *Daily Mail* had four Beatle-banged De Gaulles, strumming guitars, and singing to Sir Alec Douglas-Home, *à propos* Chancellor Erhard, 'She loves me, *oui, oui, oui*'. The cartoon was labelled 'The Paris Sound'.

Back in the City of Light, John and Paul slept till three o'clock in the afternoon. That much everybody is agreed on. From then on the stories differ. According to George in the *Daily Express*:

We stopped the traffic on the Champs-Élysées today, or rather hordes of girls did, clamouring for autographs.

John, Paul, and I had gone for a mid-afternoon stroll in the gentle sunshine when we were spotted.

Beautiful girls ran from gown shops waving paper and pens. French cabbies cursed and waved their fists as we were engulfed.

Next we tried to sit at a kerb-side café for a drink, but it was impossible.

We ran for a taxi, a crowd followed, and a new traffic jam started.

The gendarmerie dragged people off the bonnet of the taxi and we escaped to our hotel.

Is Beatlemania starting off here? There are signs.

However, Vincent Mulchrone, the award-winning veteran reporter for the *Daily Mail*, wrote:

If Paris and the Beatles are going to have an affair, it is getting off to a slow start. You can't blame Paris. She was warm and inviting this morning. The Beatles were warm, but only because they were asleep, and stayed that way until three o'clock in the afternoon.

Admittedly, George Harrison was astir early, but John Lennon and Paul McCartney slumbered on until frantic photographers forced them at lens point into the Champs-Élysées.

The decision to let them venture thus far (all of 500 yards) was taken at the highest level by the Beatle top brass, men who tend to reminisce over battles at English stage doors and talk gravely of 'security problems'.

They needn't have worried. Either the Champs-Élysées was not in mobbing mood today, or Beatlemania is still, like Britain's entry into the Common Market, a problem the French prefer to put off for a while.

Exactly three girls asked them for autographs. One was English.

The accuracy of the reports is a moot point. However, figuring prominently in the pictures of the Beatles at a café table in the Champs-Élysées are two reporters for a British women's magazine.

The same night in their suite Epstein is telling them they will have to rehearse the following afternoon for the opening at the Olympia.

'Why?' asks John. 'There's no need to rehearse. We always do the same thing. Besides, the only thing they know here is "She Loves You".'

Ringo asks if they can go out tonight.

'No,' says Epstein, 'you have to choose between staying up at night or working.'

'Good,' says George. 'We'll just stay up at night and chuck the working.'

The cinema in Versailles where the Beatles were to make their French début was playing two Dracula films. They arrived at the stage door in a borrowed Cadillac, as their Austin Princess had broken down in the Paris traffic. They remained in their dressing-room while waiting to go on.

Epstein went across the road to a café for a drink. 'Did you see the story in the *New Yorker*?' he asked. 'I thought it was very good, except for that part where it called me round-faced.' He was interrupted by Derek Taylor, who wanted to know why the Beatles slept so much. 'My office wants to know what they're doing in Paris, so they'd better be doing something,' he said.

Shortly after midnight the Beatles were introduced, but then a juggling act came on stage. Finally, they appeared and did their usual act with no concesssions to the fact that their audience didn't understand English. Trini Lopez, an American singer, had received a great deal of applause earlier when he had said a few words in French, but the Beatles didn't follow his lead. At one point, a young man dressed as the French singer Johnny Hallyday came on stage and was carried off by Mal Evans, a hulking giant of a man who transports the Beatles' amplifiers and drums. It wasn't until John started singing 'Twist and Shout' that the audience really came to life. '*Un autre, un autre,*' they called, and Paul stepped up to belt out a bopped-up version of a Little Richard song.

Back at the hotel they toasted their first show in France. John had bought a 35-mm. camera, and now they all had them, and were hopping around taking pictures of one another and drinking champagne. In the midst of this a call from New York came for Epstein. 'I Want to Hold Your Hand' had sold a million and a half records in the United States, and after three weeks on the American charts it was now number one. It was only the third time a record had risen so quickly and the first time it had ever been done by a non-American artist. As soon as Epstein had hung up, another call came through from Detroit, offering ten thousand dollars for one appearance. When Epstein told them the news, Paul climbed on Mal Evans's back and rode piggyback all round the suite.

The next afternoon at the Olympia they were interviewed by the British press. George was with the *Daily Express*, John the *Daily Mirror,* and Ringo was talking to Stephen Coulter, the veteran Paris correspondent of the *Sunday Times*. Coulter had just come from Cap Ferrat where he had interviewed Somerset Maugham on his ninetieth birthday. 'I'm not very *au courant* on the Beatles,' he said to Ringo. 'Now, tell me, how long do you think you will last?'

An hour later the Beatles performed for an audience of

students while French television filmed their reaction. The degree of audience participation seemed to depend on whether the TV lights were on, and the students rose and fell like waves.

Out in front of the Olympia Tim Green of *Life* was still trying to get a story. He was watching crowds of young Parisians in Beatle wigs taking their pictures on an automatic photo-machine that had been set up in the entrance. 'We just came over from London for lunch,' he said, 'but now they are number one the editors are pressing for a cover and God knows what we're going to do.'

That evening for the opening night *tout Paris* was in the audience. Backstage, photographers, many of whom had just returned from covering the Pope's visit to the Holy Land, were amusing themselves with Beatle wigs. After waiting two hours they started to get restive, and finally, fifteen minutes before they were scheduled on stage, the Beatles arrived, ran to their dressing-room – and locked the door.

The photographers exploded and knocked on the door. It was opened by the Beatles' driver and Mal Evans. Both are over six feet tall. The battle of the Olympia was joined. A camera went spinning in the air amid a volley of Gallic curses.

Inside the dressing-room was Maureen Cleave, who had been at the George V, and entered with the Beatles. In the excitement George blamed the fight on Brian Sommerville and threw a glass of orange juice at him.

Outside, the fight has subsided and several photographers are let into the dressing-room to take pictures. Maureen Cleave has now moved into the bar, where Vincent Mulchrone is standing like an imperturbable monument, calmly sipping champagne.

'I managed to get past the police just now,' says Miss Cleave worriedly. 'But if I go into the theatre to see the show I don't know how I'll get backstage again. I don't have a pass, like you, Vincent.'

Mulchrone looks down at her, takes another sip of champagne, and replies: 'Don't worry my dear, you may pose as my mother.'

During the performance the amplifiers break down three times. 'These photographers must have sabotaged the system,' says George, quite audibly, on stage. John, making a concession to the audience, says the only words he knows in French: '*Je me lève à sept heures.*' 'How barbaric,' says a young lady in the first row, also quite audibly.

After the show the back-stage entrance was guarded by two dozen policemen. Standing by the barrier, trying to get in to speak with the Beatles, were representatives of CBS, AP, the *Daily Mail*, and the *Evening Standard*, as well as their recording manager, George Martin.

The representative of the Associated Press was telling the policeman that if *he* didn't get in nobody in the world would know about the Beatles' opening in Paris.

'Paris knows, Monsieur,' said the *flic* and shrugged.

Suddenly, in a rush of French photographers Sommerville came near the barrier. 'I'm taking these boys back to London,' he yelled as he was carried away on a wave of photographers.

In the dressing-room, Epstein, wearing his overcoat and a polka-dotted scarf, was adjusting a new Borsalino hat. An executive of a Swedish record company came over and told him they must talk in London.

'Billy J. is coming to Sweden,' says Epstein.

'I know,' says the man, 'but anyway, we must talk.'

'Yes, I know,' says Epstein wearily. 'The Beatles, always the Beatles. They don't know it but I cried tonight, I really did. They never noticed, but I cried.'

In the Paris office of the *Daily Mail* Maureen Cleave was saying she thought the Beatles' manners were 'atrocious' and asking if anybody knew how much money they were getting for their appearance in Paris. Suddenly, the teletype rang with a message from London:

'Is true Beatles returning here?'

The Associated Press man had put over the only story he could get: Sommerville's threat.

Maureen Cleave, Vincent Mulchrone, and the Paris correspondent of the London *Evening News* went to the George V to check the story for London. 'No, of course it isn't true,' said Paul and invited them to come into the suite where there was a party going on.

Several hours later George started to get bored. He picked up the telephone and in a serious voice told the *concierge* to come up and throw some people out. When someone expressed amazement at his behaviour he was told that the first time the Beatles had met George Martin, he had had them listen to a playback of their tapes and tell him if there was anything they didn't like. 'Well,' George had told him, 'I don't like your tie for a start.'

At five in the morning Derek Taylor came into the suite with Peter Evans, the show-business columnist, who had flown over for the night. Paul ordered some cheese sandwiches, which he sprayed with ketchup and ate; then he started to entertain the people who remained. Evans listened politely, and then suddenly, when the Beatles were occupied elsewhere, he bolted from his seat, shouted out 'Good-bye, loves,' and ran out of the door.

John had been missing for several hours. It wasn't until the next day that one learned that he had been sitting with Maureen Cleave in a café discussing the opening of the Beatles in Paris.

The next day, *France-Soir*, under the headline: '*Les Beatles:*

des vieux zazous rénovés par le yé-yé', said the Beatles were simply a reincarnation of the '*zazous*' groups of French juvenile delinquents after the war. 'Their *yé-yé* is the worst we have heard in four years,' the review said, 'and physically they are even more *déposés* than their music. England may need the jolt they have brought to a staid country but there is nothing that a Paris audience will less support than "*des vedettes démodées*" ' – or, as they put it in English, '*des* have-beens'. The other Paris papers printed similar reviews.

At a press conference for the British press Ringo was asked if he had read the notices in the French papers.

'I can't read French,' he replied.

BBC Interviewer: 'How important is it to succeed here?'

Paul: 'It is important to succeed anywhere.'

BBC: 'The French have not made up their minds about the Beatles. What do you think of them?'

John: 'Oh, we like the Beatles. They're gear.'

A special messenger came to the suite to deliver a petition signed by the 500 men of the First Battalion of the King's Own Regiment stationed in Berlin. Most of the men are from Liverpool and some of them had known the Beatles at home. The petition declared the Beatles were 'off-beat by 542 miles in Paris' and invited them to Berlin. It ended, 'See you at the Brandenburg Gate, *bitte, ja, ja, ja*'.

On the same day another petition arrived, this one signed by 200 girls. It called for 'John Lennon to wear his glasses on stage; George to talk more; Ringo to sing more; and Paul to keep his accent'.

This petition was one of thousands of communications from fans that filled the suite. In addition to written notes a great many took advantage of the fact that the George V telephone number is public knowledge, and the switchboard was swamped.

Sometimes the fans combined the two modes of communication:

MESSRS LENNON, MCCARTNEY, HARRISON, STARR, HOTEL GEORGE V, PARIS: KNOW YOU MUST BE FED-UP BUT PLEASE ACCEPT SHORT CALL WEDNESDAY 1115 YOUR TIME.

Or even:

PAUL MCCARTNEY HOTEL GEORGE V
SURPRISE CALL QUICK TRO 7865
MICHÈLE

Walking from the George V to the broadcasting studios of Europe Number One – the first time they have gone out unaccompanied in Paris – Paul is approached by a young girl who asks for his autograph and then:

Girl: 'Would you write to me?'
Paul: 'We're very busy.'
Girl: 'Just a few lines.'
Paul: 'You write to me first.'
Girl: 'I did, yesterday.'
Paul: 'What's your name?'
Girl: 'Adrienne.'
Paul: 'Oh, sure, I'll remember. I'll try and write.'
Girl: 'It would make me so happy.'

One night Derek Taylor changed from his usual Italianate suit into a Beatle-type Cardin jacket and arrived at the suite with several girls. A picture of the Beatles having a pillow fight had run in the *Express* and Taylor wanted to have a different type of photo. Most of the girls were British or American, and some of them worked at the Lido or the Folies Bergère.

A tall blonde from Sewickly, Pennsylvania ('it's really Pittsburgh'), is standing by the bar and wondering what she is doing at the George V.

'I guess I'm just a pick-up,' she says. 'I was sitting at this café and this man came over and asked me if I wanted to go Beatling. I think the Beatles are great, so I went.'

Someone asks whether she works at the Lido.

'No,' she replies, 'I don't work at all. I guess you could call me a student. I studied at the Sorbonne for two days but it was all in French. I guess I'll just have to learn some more before I go back.'

A Canadian girl in a bulky sweater who works at the Casino de Paris and has a voice like Marilyn Monroe walks over. She sips her drink and looks at Paul and George talking to several girls. 'They seem so unsure of themselves,' she says. 'They're always looking at each other. I guess they're just very, very young.'

On the ride back from a picture session someone suggests going to a *bistro* on the Left Bank.

'Why?' asks George.

'Because Paris has some of the best restaurants in the world.'

'Who says so?' he replies.

Except for a meal at a restaurant that featured sponge-rubber breasts on the wall and phallic dinner rolls, the Beatles had all their meals in their suite at the George V. Most of the time they ordered pork or fish. The first day Paul asked for banana pancakes which were served *flambés*. They liked them and at £5 a portion they ordered them every day. They were always given the same waiter because of his fluency in English. 'You speak with such a funny accent,' George told him one night. Another time he told the waiter that they were fourth in Hong Kong.

'That's an important market,' explained Paul.

A French newspaper said that in addition to playing the guitar both Brigitte Bardot and the Beatles washed their hair every day.

Jane Asher came to Paris for a few days and stayed at a small hotel near the Sorbonne. It was her first trip and she wanted to see the city, but Paul said she might be recognized and that she should stay in the suite at the George V while the Beatles were performing at the Olympia.

'That's typical of Paul,' she remarked. 'It's so silly of me to stay at the hotel. It's just that he's so insecure. For instance, he keeps saying he's not interested in the future, but he must be because he says it so often. The trouble is, he wants the fans' adulation and mine too. He's so selfish; it's his biggest fault. He can't see that my feelings for him are real and that the fans' are fantasy. Of course, it's the trouble with all the boys. When I first met them I liked them all. Then, when I found out I liked Paul more, the others became angry with me.'

'When will you make a new record?' the Beatles were asked by an interviewer.

'Don't know,' said John. 'We'll have to write it first.'

They never got around to writing a song for themselves in Paris although they did record the instrumental track for 'You Can't Do That', a song they had already written. What they *did* do was to finish a song they had started which was to be recorded by another of Epstein's clients, Billy J. Kramer.

It is called 'One and One is Two' and it was finished in their suite at the George V one night after a performance at the Olympia. Paul, still in his stage make-up, sat at a piano they had installed in one of the sitting-rooms. John, wearing a polo-necked sweater and sun-glasses, sat at a table playing a guitar. A microphone leading from a tape-recorder was strapped to a floor lamp. Paul started singing:

'One and one is two.
What am I to do
Now that I'm in love with you?'

Occasionally George stuck his head in the door to listen. 'Can't you take one of the "one and one is two"'s out?' he asks at one point. 'Can't you do something with "do" or "Jew"?'

'I'm a lonely Jew,' says John. 'How's that?'

Ringo wanders around, says he is bored, and asks George to go with him to a night club to hear some jazz. Meanwhile, John is considering George's suggestion.

'That bit does get on me nerves. Let's see, "true", "blue", "it's a point of view" . . .'

John starts to play on a harmonica and to fool around. Paul remains serious. They change places. John sits at the piano and Paul at the guitar. Paul sings into the microphone. John bangs at the chords on the piano, still wearing his sun-glasses. He has now put his leather cap on.

'Paul bought a Bob Dylan record,' he says, 'and he was wearing this exact cap on the cover. He even had the button open like mine. Everybody will think I copied it from him.'

After taping the song three times, John is satisfied, but Paul feels they have yet to get a good take. The words to the song, written on George V note-paper, lie spread over the suite among the hundreds of letters from fans. John says that they once recorded a song in a bathroom and ended with Ringo flushing the toilet.

'It was a new sound, but our music publisher, Dick James, cut it out. He missed the whole thing.'

Paul has been revising some of the lyrics. When he finishes he calls John and they sing the song again. Paul then prefaces the tape with a message for Dick James, who is expecting the tape in London the next morning.

'I guess this is okay,' he says to James on the tape.

'Billy J. is finished when he gets this song,' says John.

Ringo and George had gone off to hear jazz. After an hour George said to their driver, who accompanied them, 'Feed me and take me home.' Shortly afterwards he came back to the suite with Ringo and went to bed.

Ringo wandered over to the piano and started improvising blues.

'My mother was a barmaid,' he sang, 'my father was a painter . . .

'I started to be an engineer but I banged me thumb the first day. I became a drummer because it was the only thing I could do. But whenever I hear another drummer I know I'm no good. John learned me the song I sing. I can only play on the off beat because John can't keep up on the rhythm guitar. I'm no good on the technical things but I'm good with all the motions, swinging my head, like. That's because I love to dance but you can't do that on drums.

'I remember when I first met the boys in Hamburg. Everybody used to talk about them because they did things like John going on stage with a toilet seat around his neck. They were living in an empty cinema called the Bambi which they called "the Pit". I was living at a hotel, because I was with a group called the Raving Texans.

'Back in Liverpool, whenever Pete Best would get sick I would take over. Sometimes it was at lunch time. I remember once Neil got me out of bed and I had no kit. I got up on stage with only cymbals and gradually Pete's kit started arriving piece by piece.

'I figure we're good for another four years. I don't want to invest me money in stocks or anything. I just want to have it and draw twenty or thirty quid a week. The main thing is, I don't ever want to go back to work.

'I don't want to boast but when we were playing in Liverpool I was one of the two best drummers in town. We used to play for ten bob a night. I don't think I could ever do that again.'

One night Alun Owen came to dinner to discuss the film. Paul said he didn't like the way he talked to the Beatles as if he had never left Liverpool, but to Jane with an Oxford accent.

Owen and the film's producer Walter Shenson told them they would have to be on the set at a specific time each day.

'What if we're not?' said George.

'Then there won't be a film,' he was informed.

Sommerville told them that the wife of the British Ambassador in Paris, Lady Dixon, had invited them to dinner at the Embassy.

'Don't be soft,' said Paul. 'Doesn't she know we have three shows that night?'

The New Jimmy's, Paris's most chic *discothèque,* had a 'Beatlemanie Night'. A sign inside the door read: '*Tenue–Cheveux et Pull "Beatles"* '.

A large crowd of young Parisians turned up, many of them wearing Beatle wigs. The Beatles came but after a few minutes Sommerville advised them to leave. 'I want to keep them remote,' he said. 'Establish your idol and keep it at a distance. I'm convinced that's what accounts for the survival of the monarchy. If we have too many occasions like Wimbledon, what will the girls have to look forward to?'

An American reporter asked why all the Beatles' songs had the words 'I', 'me', or 'you' in them.

'Should it be "I Want to Hold Its Hand",' said John, 'or "She loves them"?'

A reporter for the fashion page of the *New York Times* asked who did their hair in France.

'Nobody does it in England.'

She then wanted to know where the style had developed.

'Well, let's see,' said George. 'I think it was in Germany...'

At two o'clock one afternoon two reporters for American newspapers are waiting in Sommerville's room to interview the Beatles. They have an appointment for one o'clock but the boys are still asleep.

'Let's see,' says one of the men. 'Harrison's been to the States; let's start with him.'

The Beatles enter in dressing-gowns: Ringo in bright red, John and Paul in blue, wool; George in blue and black silk.

The journalists ask Paul how he liked the States and Paul points to George and says he is the one who has been there.

'Okay,' says one of the men, 'let's get it straight. Why don't you just introduce yourselves?' They do this and then the other man asks about their hair-do.

'You mean hair-don't,' says John.

'Well,' says George, 'we were coming out of a swimming-baths in Liverpool and we liked the way it looked.'

One of the interviewers asks: 'Do you ride that Rolls-Royce all the time?'

'That "Rolls-Royce" is an Austin,' says George.

The Beatles leave to have breakfast and Sommerville tells the reporters: 'You're fortunate. That's the most serious interview they've ever given.'

'It was very sincere,' says one of the journalists.

'Well, it was early in the day,' says Sommerville.

Towards the end of their stay in Paris the American columnist Sheilah Graham asked to interview the Beatles. They were to fly to New York the following week, and Miss Graham wanted to devote her column to them a few days before they arrived.

She made several appointments to see them, which for one reason or the other were broken. Now, a few hours before she was scheduled to leave Paris, she arrived in Sommerville's suite to wait for them.

She asked Sommerville what cities they were appearing in, and as he named each one she told him that she was represented by a paper there. The Beatles were at the American

Hospital taking physical examinations required by the insurance company of their film. After Miss Graham had waited an hour Sommerville excused himself and walked into the hall.

'I wish they would hurry,' he said. 'They're so inconsiderate. I can just see them years from now writing their memoirs for the *Sunday Express* – "why didn't I listen to those who knew better?" ' He wrung his hands. 'I need complete control but every time I speak to Brian he keeps saying, "Everything's liaising". I don't know what to do. I don't have any trouble with the press. It's just the boys.'

He walked back to his suite and apologized to Miss Graham for keeping her waiting.

'That's perfectly all right,' she says, laughing. 'I've given up the Queen of England and Princess Grace for you.'

'Oh dear,' says Sommerville.

Twenty minutes later he apologizes again and tells Miss Graham that he 'hates keeping someone as famous as you waiting'.

'I'm the least famous person I know,' says Miss Graham.

They talk for several minutes more. Then Miss Graham picks up an advance copy of *Life* magazine which has a six-page story on the Beatles in it. Suddenly, the door opens and George sticks his head in.

'Why, hello, dear,' says Miss Graham, rising from her chair. 'Now, tell me quickly, which one are *you*?'

America, America, and Ed Sullivan

... I'm in acting school and want to be a singer and actress, and I know what all that travelling's like. And another thing: I've been in thirteen different houses during my life, but gradually everything gets better and better, and one day I hope to be a star ('hope's' the word) so that I can prove that I can do something too. And don't ever worry, George, about going down the ladder, because you four have got what it takes like none of the other groups have got. It's not your songs (though the words of your songs send me and bring back so many memories) or the way you stomp on the stage, or do your little solo bits on the guitar, but it's just you, you're natural, not like the others. That's why you're on top. I'm not trying to kid you, 'cause everyone has to go down sometimes, but you won't for a long time, don't worry. But the fans love you, really they do. Speaking as a fan myself, I know what it's like ... but it's great to be able to write to you like this, George, 'cause you've probably gathered you're my favourite Beatle. You put over sincerity and that counts a lot when you've got fans. I hope, by the way, that you enjoy America. Lots of people ask me if I think the Beatles will become American citizens after their stay but I know you well enough to say that you love your home (Liverpool) best, don't you, George? But of course!

Oh, well . . . I hope I can come to your birthday party as I must talk to you, George, before I go bonkers. My friend at school went to your party last year. You came with the others to pick her up at her house. It was funny, really, 'cause Paul used her 'lav' and she would'nt let her mum clean the 'lav' out until — months later, it was. It started to smell so it had to be cleaned after long last. But it was funny, 'cause she was always up in that toilet.

From a letter

After some trouble over visas with the American authorities, the Beatles received an H2 category which was above H3 (trainees) but below H1 for 'persons of distinguished merit and ability'. Their work permits were valid 'as long as unemployed American citizens capable of performing this work cannot be found'.

A few days before the Beatles were to leave for the United States it was announced that in addition to appearing on the Ed Sullivan television programme they would give two concerts at Carnegie Hall. Within hours after the announcement was made all the tickets were gone. They were being paid $10,500 for two shows at Carnegie Hall, and the New York impresario Sidney Bernstein offered them $25,000 plus $5,000 for the British Cancer Fund if they would give one performance in the mammoth Madison Square Garden. Epstein refused.

'Don't they realize,' said Bernstein, 'this isn't show business, it's history?'

Entering into the spirit of the occasion, the *Daily Express* revealed that according to high Washington sources the Beatles would be invited to the White House.

Two of the Beatles' records had been distributed in America a year earlier and had failed to make an impression. Then the steady publicity in the British national press had been picked up by the London offices of the American news media. *Time, Newsweek,* and the *New York Times*, as well as NBC and CBS, all had stories on the Beatles, treating them as news phenomena rather than show-business personalities.

In order to ensure that this gratuitous publicity was not dissipated, Epstein persuaded Capitol, the Beatles' American recording company, to spend fifty thousand dollars for what they called a 'crash publicity program'.

They plastered five million 'The Beatles Are Coming' stickers on telephone poles, washroom walls, and other appropriate places throughout the country. They distributed the record the Beatles had made in London to every disc jockey in the country. They issued a four-page newspaper on the Beatles and sent out a million copies. They photographed their top executives wearing Beatle wigs and distributed 'Be a Beatle Booster' badges to all their employees. They offered Beatle haircuts free to all their female employees and persuaded Janet Leigh to get one. They even tried, unsuccessfully, to bribe a University of Washington cheer-leader into holding up a card reading 'The Beatles Are Coming' to the television cameras at the Rose Bowl.

'There was,' said Capitol Vice-President Voyle Gilmore, 'a lot of hype.'

On the morning of their departure from London, the *Daily Mirror*, in an article written by Donald Zec, said the Beatles were a passing phase as contrasted to Cliff Richard who had been studying his craft for years, but who nevertheless told Mr Zec he thought his colleagues from Liverpool were 'fab'. The national papers also carried reviews of Edward Albee's *Who's Afraid of Virginia Woolf?*, which had opened the night before. 'Why must we always look to America for excitement like this?' one of them asked.

Four thousand girls who had arrived at London Airport too early to read the papers gave the Beatles a screaming farewell as their plane left London.

Shortly afterwards, radio station WMCA in New York made the first of a series of announcements: 'It is now 6.30 a.m. Beatle time. They left London thirty minutes ago; they're out over the Atlantic Ocean headed for New York. The temperature is 32 Beatle degrees.'

Aboard the plane, the Beatles, accompanied by John's wife, Cynthia, and Epstein, sat in the first-class compartment. Their fellow passengers included George Harrison (no relation), a columnist for the *Liverpool Echo* and *Liverpool Daily Post*; Harry Benson, a photographer for the *Daily Express*; and Maureen Cleave of the *Evening Standard*. Also aboard was Phil Spector, a constantly sun-glassed American who is responsible for earning millions of dollars by writing such songs as 'Da Doo Ron Ron'.

I was in the economy section of the plane with the Beatles' road manager, Neil Aspinall; his assistant Mal Evans; the photographer Bob Freeman, who was to record the trip for Epstein and the *Daily Mirror*; the photographer Dezo Hoffmann; as well as representatives of several other British publications and some British television stations. At one point during the trip Epstein came back and passed out a list of seventeen names who were 'press contacts' in every corporation with whom the Beatles would deal, from the Columbia Broadcasting System to the Hotel Deauville in Miami Beach.

In addition to the journalists there were several British manufacturers, who, tired of not being able to speak with Epstein in London, had decided that a plane 30,000 feet above the Atlantic was the best place to do business. Several of them sent products up to him with a note asking for an endorsement. They were all politely refused. Meanwhile, the Beatles relaxed, laughed at the stewardess's life-saving instructions, and wondered about the reception awaiting them.

Paul was pessimistic. 'Since America has always had everything,' he asked Spector, 'why should we be over there making money? They've got their own groups. What are we going to give them that they don't already have?'

Maureen Cleave turned round and told Paul not to worry. 'You'll go like a bomb in America.'

'What?' asked Spector.

'I said they'd go like a bomb,' said Miss Cleave.

Someone came over to explain that what in England was a sign of confidence meant exactly the opposite in America, and the plane continued on its journey.

Harry Benson came back to tell several journalists that the Beatles liked him because 'I just play like I'm a daft soppy ha'porth'. He had tipped the stewardess to be allowed to take pictures exclusively during the trip and now he began lining the Beatles up for photos against the Manhattan skyline outside the window. When the plane began to descend all they could see were the two family houses of Queens that surround Kennedy International Airport.

'Hey!' said Benson. 'I think we've come to the wrong place.'

Any doubts that the Beatles (to say nothing of Benson) entertained were immediately settled when the plane came to a stop. Outside, what looked like the entire teenage population of the Greater New York area were waiting. From the window of the plane they seemed like a photo mural against the blue sky.

The mural quickly came to life when the plane's door was opened. The shouts of a hundred photographers crouched on a hydraulic crane blended antiphonically with the wailing wall of pubescence. As the Beatles reached the bottom of the stairway, a policeman who had been assigned to take them in hand came over and told them not to smile or wave 'or you'll excite them'! Then, turning to his companion, he remarked, 'Boy, could they use a haircut!'

Everyone leaving the plane was handed a 'Beatle Kit' consisting of a wig, a button saying 'I like the Beatles', and an autographed photo. As the Beatles posed for pictures on the tarmac a Pan American Airways executive was trying to cover their BEAtle bags with the 'Beatle Kits'. During this lull an airport employee came over and asked for their autographs. When he received them he ran to show it to a few friends.

'Hey, look!' he said. 'Twenty bucks!'

It was 1.20 p.m. Beatle time.

The press room on the first floor of the arrivals building was jammed. From outside came the screams of the thousand teenagers who had chosen the customs section as their observation point. While the Beatles were declaring their baggage the press waited expectantly.

'Do you realize,' said one reporter, 'that if "Beatle" were in the dictionary it would come between "beatitude", meaning consummate bliss or blessedness, and "beat note", which is a note whose frequency equals the difference in the frequency of the two vibrators?'

Outside, several of the girls tried to hurl themselves over a retaining wall as the Beatles passed beneath.

Brian Sommerville, who had arrived in New York two days earlier to 'liaise' with the press, was now surrounded by them. A photographer from a New York paper that had bought a serial on the Beatles' lives from an English paper was complaining he couldn't get any pictures of them. The British press corps was complaining that the police wouldn't let them in the press room without New York credentials. A policeman tried to throw out a promotion executive from Capitol Records who didn't have an identification badge. From the back of the room came word that two girls had fainted outside.

'This,' said Sommerville, 'has got entirely out of control.'

The Beatles are led into the press room where they stand on a platform talking and smiling quietly. Beneath them photographers cry: 'Down in front . . . gimme some room . . . whatsa matta . . . I can't see . . . please, down . . . more . . . no more . . . be a sport . . . hey, Beatles, look ovahere . . . whodda the left to rights . . . which one is George?'

Finally, Sommerville steps to the microphone. 'Would the photographers please be quiet now so the reporters can ask questions? Please.' This is met by cries of anguish from the photographers.

Sommerville grabs the microphone. 'Ladies and gentlemen, this is ridiculous! Hold up your hands, and I'll recognize you one at a time. If you won't be quiet we'll just stand here until you are. All right then!' he says. 'Shut up! Just shut up!'

The Beatles join in. 'Yeah, yeah, everybody shut up,' says John. Reporters applaud. Somebody asks, 'Aren't you embarrassed by all this lunacy?'

'No,' says John. 'It's crazy.'

'Will you sing something for us?' asks a reporter.

'We need money first,' says John.

'How do you account for your success?'

'We have a press agent.'

'What is your ambition?'

'To come to America.'

'Do you hope to get haircuts?'

'We had one yesterday.'

'Do you hope to take anything home with you?'

'The Rockefeller Center.'

'Are you part of a social rebellion against the older generation?'

'It's a dirty lie.'

'What about the movement in Detroit to stamp out Beatles?'

'We have a campaign of our own to stamp out Detroit.'

'What do you think of Beethoven?'

'I love him,' says Ringo, 'especially his poems.'

At the back of the press room a woman reporter is talking on the phone: 'They are absolutely too cute for words and America is just going to love them.'

Epstein is being interviewed by a man with a tape-recorder:

Shakespearian Beatle: Ringo in 'A Midsummer Night's Dream'

Waiting for a Beatle

Three Beatles in Paris

New York welcome

Press call

Police quell Beatle riot with bullets

Washington tour de force

Triumphant return to London

Offstage

John and Cynthia Lennon

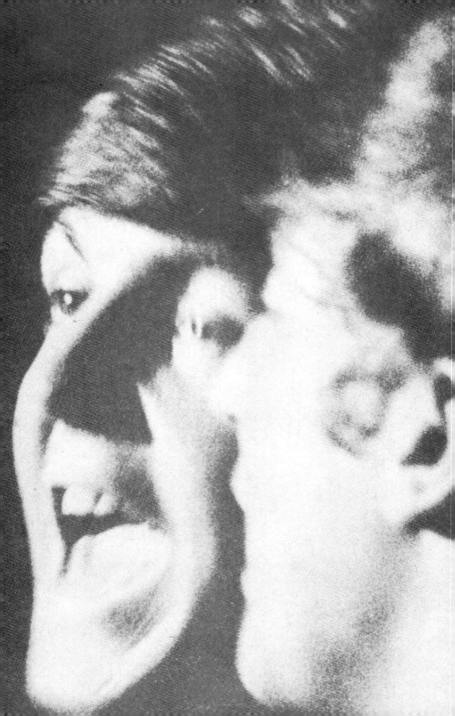

Man: 'I'm speaking with Brian Epstein, the Beatles' manager. Brian, tell me: how was the reception?'

Epstein: 'Great, just great . . . the best reception ever.'

Man: 'Would you say it was the best reception ever?'

Outside four Cadillac limousines are waiting. Within ten seconds of the end of the press conference each contains a Beatle and is in motion. A policeman is shouting at the first chauffeur, 'Get out of here, buddy, if you want to get out alive!'

On the Long Island expressway leading into Manhattan, the caravan of Cadillacs is overtaken by a powder-blue Ford convertible that races alongside. A young man hangs out of the back window, waving a red blanket.

'So this is America!' says Ringo. 'They all seem out of their minds.'

A white convertible drives up with the word BEETLES written in the dust on either side. Brian Sommerville turns to George and says, 'Did you see that, George?'

George looks at the convertible with its emblem in the dust and says, 'They misspelled "Beatles".'

Half-way into Manhattan a crimson convertible drives up next to Ringo's limousine. 'Ringo, Ringo,' shout the passengers, 'we go Ringo.' The girls squeal and the boy behind the wheel momentarily loses his grip, nearly smashing into the Cadillac's rear door.

Ringo rolls the window down. 'Hi, kids,' he calls.

'Yeah, yeah, yeah,' yell the kids.

'What's new?' asks Ringo.

'We love you, Ringo, we love you,' one girl screams. 'Oh – I'm about ready to die, DIE!'

'Don't do that,' says Ringo and rolls the window up.

At 63rd Street and Third Avenue, while waiting for a traffic light, a young lady shouts into George's car:

'How does one go about meeting a Beatle?'

George leans out of his window.

'One says hello,' he says, but the light changes and the Cadillac lurches ahead towards Fifth Avenue and the Hotel Plaza.

As Rome cherishes the Colosseum and Paris the Arc de Triomphe as symbols of a more glorious day, so New York feels about the Hotel Plaza. Generations of débutantes have danced in its *fin de siècle* ballrooms, and the most dissonant sound to be heard is the rare one of too much vermouth pouring into a martini.

Now the silver-haired ladies who cling to the Plaza like its reputation were looking askance. There were screaming hordes of adolescent girls surrounding the fountain where Scott and Zelda had bathed at midnight.

The Plaza management was petrified. Months ago they had accepted the Beatles' reservations, as businessmen, under their own names, checking only that they were 'financially responsible'. When the truth dawned, one of the Plaza executives went on the radio and offered the Beatles to any hotel in New York that wanted them.

During the first hour at the hotel the Beatles watched films of their arrival at the airport on television and posed for photographers. One of them asked John to lie on a bed and display his boots.

'Oh, no, please don't do that at the Plaza!' pleaded a distraught hotel official. 'That's not the image we want to project!'

'Don't worry,' said John, 'we'll buy the bed.'

To all Front Service:

During the stay of the Beatles at the Plaza Hotel I want extreme caution by all elevator operators as to the type of people you take upstairs to the 12th, 13th, and 14th floors.

Several girls climbed twelve flights of stairs to the wing where the Beatles' suite was located. In self-defence the Plaza hired guards to be on round-the-clock duty, and a desk was set up at the entrance to their wing.

'Why did you pick the Plaza?' a reporter asks George.

'I don't know,' he replies. 'I didn't pick it. Our manager did. All I can tell you is that the food is awful.'

In the hallway, Gail Cameron, a *Life* reporter, waited with a photographer. 'Listen,' she said to a press aide, 'I don't want to interview them, I just want their autograph for my managing editor – he told me not to come back without it.'

Several doors away is Brian Sommerville's suite. He is in the bedroom in tears. He has just had a fight with Epstein over the room arrangements and has been fired. 'I plan to return to London on the first available plane,' he says dramatically.

On the coffee table in the sitting-room lies a box of candy with a telegram pasted to it, reading: 'I hope you like these better than jelly-babies. Good luck – Kitty Curowsky.' Sitting on the sofa are Thomas Whiteside of the *New Yorker* and Alfred Aronowitz of the *Saturday Evening Post*.

'I don't feel very well,' says Whiteside, looking pale.

'Man,' says Aronowitz, a nervous, bearded type, 'don't you sense the excitement here?'

Sommerville has asked the hotel to put all of the Beatles' calls through to his room and the telephone keeps ringing. A radio station wants to tape thirty seconds of Ringo's conversation. A manufacturer wants to produce Beatle ashtrays. 'Uh, a group of us in the Village were wondering if the boys ...' A promoter in Hawaii wants to book the Beatles for

97

a tour there. 'Uh, this is Miss Grey of Capitol records. Could you have the Beatles call me at home tonight . . . ?'

Sommerville re-enters the sitting-room. His argument with Epstein had been resolved. He is staying on.

The phone rings again. A charity organization wants to photograph a little girl in a wheel chair shaking hands with one of the Beatles. 'Oh dear, now that *is* a problem,' Sommerville says after hanging up. 'I always hate to have the boys photographed under those circumstances. You know what I mean – sort of gives the impression of a freak meeting a freak.'

They sit in silence for a minute. Then Aronowitz says: 'Listen, man, I don't want to talk to them. I just want to stand there and get images.'

'I'm definitely not well,' says Whiteside and leaves.

Lying opened on a table in the Beatles' suite is a note – one of hundreds, most of them still sealed.

Brooklyn

Dear Beatles,

Here are some questions we hope you will answer for us:

1. John; Do you and your wife have any children?

2. Paul; Is it true that you have a special girl back in Liverpool?

3. To all four; What do you think of American girls?

4. To all four; Do you have an interest in your fans?

5. To all four; When are your birthdays?

6. Ringo; Where did you get your rings and how long have you played drums?

7. To all four; Do you see any difference in American fans and those of other countries?

8. George; Who picks out your clothes and haircuts?

9. To all four; What American do you admire?

10. To all four; Do you enjoy writing your music and what mood do you do it in?

11. To all four; What is your religion?

Sincerely yours,
Gayle

'We get 12,000 letters a day,' says Ringo. 'Yeah,' adds John, 'and we're going to answer every one.'

Neil Aspinall sits in a corner signing pictures of the Beatles. He has perfected their signatures, and these are being kept in anticipation of future requests. The door opens, and a New York disc jockey, called Murray the K, comes in with the Ronettes, an American recording group of three exotic-looking girls.

'We met the Beatles in London,' they say as if they are singing it.

In his room Sommerville is having dinner. One of the private guards walks in and introduces himself as 'Hughie'. As Sommerville eats, Hughie pours himself a drink and sits down. 'Say, Brian,' he says, 'Last night I was at the Waldorf, where I had the honour of guarding the President. I was on the dais and everybody had to show me their pass to leave, even to go to the men's room. It was a great honour. I even had to wear a tuxedo. Of course I still had my gun.'

Sommerville congratulates him and places a call to Lady Ormsby Gore, the wife of the British Ambassador in Washington. She has invited the Beatles to the embassy after their performance in Washington on Tuesday.

He gets her on the telephone. 'We turned down Lady Dixon in Paris, you know,' he tells her. 'Bad marks in our copybook.' He says that 'Harold Macmillan can't wait to hear how we went over; he's breathless' and that 'Sir Winston sent the boys a cigar the other day to get an autograph for his niece.' After she has invited him to 'just a small dance' at the Embassy, Sommerville laughs politely and asks, 'Are you having trouble selling tickets? Why don't you auction off their autographs?'

A short time later George developed a sore throat and the hotel doctor ordered him to bed. A German measles epidemic had been declared in New York that day and the journalists descended on Sommerville's suite. After assuring them that George was not seriously ill, he ordered them out, but promised to meet the British press in the Oak Bar.

'Can we see the Beatles?' asked one of the journalists.

'Certainly not,' said Sommerville. 'My job is to keep you press boys away from them.'

Outside, on the street, behind police barricades, the girls are keeping their vigil. The sight of a shadow in the window – any window, any floor – incites hysteria. To keep warm they sing:

'London Bridge is falling down,

. . . 'cause we've got the Beatles.'

Everybody who walks out of the door is asked, 'Did you see them?' 'Did you touch them?' A policeman comes out, and one of them yells: 'He touched a Beatle! I saw him!' Instantly he is covered with screaming, shrieking girls.

The waiters at the Plaza have been given orders to ask guests to remove Beatle wigs while in the lobby. In the Palm Court a violinist declines a request to play a medley of the Beatles' songs. He says the violin is not the proper instrument. The *Herald-Tribune* asks Kay Thompson, author of *Eloise*, to write about what is happening.

In the Oak Bar, a reporter on the London *Daily Mirror* tells his colleagues of the British press that 'It's about time to start bursting these boys' balloons. Their heads are getting too big'.

At about one-thirty in the morning, after somewhat consoling the British journalists by giving them the news about the embassy ball, Sommerville went for a stroll around the block. As he re-entered the Plaza at the 58th Street door he was stopped by a guard who asked what floor he was going to.

'Twelve,' replied Sommerville.

'I'm sorry, sir,' said the guard, conscious of where he was, 'but they've got some sort of beetles staying up there. Could you show me some identification?'

The next morning is cold and rainy but this does not deter nearly one hundred of the faithful from maintaining their barricaded vigil on the Fifth Avenue side of the hotel.

On the twelfth floor George is still ill in bed. The *Express* wants to get a picture of him with a thermometer in his mouth. Chris Wells of *Life* is standing in the corridor explaining to Aspinall that 'We can only use a picture if it's exclusive. Couldn't we get them doing anything exclusively?' John Zimmerman, a photographer specializing in colour, is worried about the special equipment he has brought to shoot a cover for the *Saturday Evening Post*. 'It's worth $100,000,' he says. 'So the magazine is paying $50 a day for a suite to store it and a Burns guard to watch that nobody steals it – while I wait for these guys.' Another photographer, called Joe Covello, has turned Sommerville's sitting-room into a studio in order to shoot a cover for *Newsweek*. He has planned to pose the Beatles together but because of George's illness he settles for individual pictures.

While he is photographing Ringo, Sommerville walks in from the bedroom, where he has been on the phone. 'How can I make arrangements for Jackson, Mississippi,' he says, 'when I don't even know where it is?' Someone hands him a bouquet of flowers for Cynthia Lennon. A reporter called Mike Hennessy, of the British magazine *Today*, asks to interview Cynthia. Sommerville says he can't.

He then turns to the other photographers and reporters in the room and, waving the flowers, tells them he has made arrangements to photograph the Beatles at the boat-house in Central Park. 'Now remember, boys,' he admonishes them, 'you won't tell anybody where they are going, it's in your interest not to tell anyone.'

In the bedroom, Brown Megs, the public relations man for Capitol Records, is making arrangements with the police.

'Of course, officer,' he is saying, 'I can tell *you* where they're going but please don't let any of the fans know.'

At the other end of the twelfth floor, safely removed from the frenzy, was Epstein's suite. It was tastefully decorated in beige and white. His bedroom looked out on Central Park, and the sitting-room the fountain and Fifth Avenue. On the table 'were copies of *Show* and the *New Yorker*, as well as *Cashbox* and *Billboard*.

While he was in New York, Epstein used his suite as an office. He was sitting there now, dictating a memo to Wendy Hanson, an elegant blonde who was serving as his secretary during the period in New York. It was the proper ambiance for dealing with important matters of high finance. The only disturbing notes were the constant screams of 'Yeah, yeah, yeah' reaching the suite through the closed windows.

Shortly afterwards the Beatles (or rather John, Paul, and Ringo), having posed for photographers at the edge of the lake in Central Park; on a rock with the skyline in the background; with the daughter of one of the *Daily Express* correspondents with the skyline in the background; and driving a landau ditto, went into the boat-house to eat cheeseburgers, drink malted milks, and speak with reporters.

As John sat down to his cheeseburger, a reporter for Associated Press, cigarette dangling from his mouth, took out his pad, looked up, and said: 'Listen, I'm not too familiar with all of this. What city are you from again?'

After they had finished talking to the reporters, the Beatles were put into two limousines and driven up the east side of Central Park to see Harlem and down the west side of the Park to the CBS studio at 53rd Street to rehearse for the Ed Sullivan show.

Outside the theatre were a number of girls wearing yellow sweatshirts carrying the emblem 'WMCA Good Guys' printed on them (the Good Guys are disc jockeys on that station who had been pushing the Beatles). There was also a boy in a white sweatshirt which was labelled 'WQXR Bad Guys'. (This is the local classical music station.) A non-affiliated young man simply carried a sign reading 'Alonzo Tuske Hates the Beatles'.

Inside, the floor of the stage was painted blue, and there were half a dozen large white arrows pointing to the place where the Beatles would sing. Explaining the significance of this, the programme's scenic designer, Bill Bohnert, said 'I was attempting to symbolize the fact that the Beatles are *here*.'

The Beatles, with Aspinall standing in for George, rehearsed only for camera angles and whispered their songs. This was rather disappointing to Kathy and Nancy Cronkite – the daughters of the CBS newsman, Walter Cronkite – who had been admitted to the studio to watch the rehearsal. Three CBS vice-presidents had been turned down. 'I guess they know where *they* stand now,' said a press aide.

Towards the end of the afternoon George turned up for the rehearsal. The press was assured that he would be able to take part in the show the next evening. 'He'd better be,' said Sullivan, 'or I'll put on a wig myself.'

After the rehearsal they went to a suite in the Savoy-Hilton, where George spent nine hundred dollars on a twelve-stringed guitar.

As they entered the Plaza they were enveloped in a squealing crowd of bridesmaids dressed in red velvet and white tulle. A man in a dinner jacket came over and told them to 'stop congesting the lobby'.

Later that evening they were taken on a drive around Manhattan by Capitol executives. Passing the United Nations building George said the flagpoles would be good to hang sweatshirts on. Afterwards they were taken to dinner at 21 where they ate pork chops and Ringo asked the captain, 'Do you have any vintage Coca-Cola?'

When they returned from 21, John, George, and Ringo

stayed in their suite to watch television. Paul went across Fifth Avenue to the Playboy Club. After it had closed he returned to the Plaza with an off-duty Bunny and another couple. The other man suggested they should go across the street to the Château Madrid.

At the bar, the owner, Danny Lopez, introduced Paul to Angel Riera, the musical director of the Chavales de España, who were appearing at the club. Señor Riera is from Barcelona, and he and Paul talked about New York and music.

As Paul was turning to leave, Señor Riera looked up at him and said, 'Excuse me – I'm not much good at placing accents when English is being spoken. You're German, aren't you?'

Leaving the hotel the next morning the Beatles' limousine was surrounded by almost 200 girls. The driver was forced to climb over the roof to get to the wheel. As the car started to pull away, someone asked John if he 'minded all this'. 'No,' he replied, 'it's not our car.'

An audience consisting mainly of teenage girls had been invited to watch the rehearsal for that evening's show as well as the taping of two additional songs for the programme in three weeks' time. They were reasonably quiet until Ringo's drums were rolled on stage. Then they began to scream. Before the Beatles appeared, Sullivan came on stage and asked the audience to give their attention to all the other fine performers besides the Beatles who were appearing, because if they didn't he would call in a barber. Then he said 'Our city – indeed, the country – has never seen anything like these four young men from Liverpool. Ladies and gentlemen, the Beatles!'

What happened to the audience next led a writer in the *New York Herald-Tribune* the following day to compare it with 'that terrible screech the BMT Astoria train makes as it turns east near 59th Street and Seventh Avenue'.

While the Beatles rehearsed, Cynthia Lennon stood in the

back of the theatre talking to Maureen Cleave. Cynthia wanted to go shopping but was afraid to go out alone. 'The fans here seem a bit wackier than in England,' she said. A fan who happened to be standing near by overheard, and ten minutes later came back with a huge parcel.

'There's no need for you to go shopping now,' she said as she presented her with a present for their six-month-old son – a 'Barracuda Atomic Sub'.

When the rehearsal and taping ended, Sullivan stood on the stage. 'It warms me to hear such enthusiasm,' he said.

'I'm going to be sick,' said a cameraman in the background.

Someone asked Sullivan about the comment of his musical director Ray Bloch that had appeared in the *New York Times* that morning. Bloch had told the *Times*: 'The only thing that's different is the hair, as far as I can see. I give them a year.'

Sullivan called Bloch over.

'Now, Ray,' he said, 'you can't say things like that.'

'They asked me how long I thought the Beatles would be making this kind of money,' replied Bloch, an elegant little man in a goatee, 'and I said about a year. Of course, I meant that they would then make a movie and make *more* money.'

On the other side of the stage a young man carrying a stenographic pad walked over to a CBS press aide. He worked for *Time* magazine and had been sent to New York from Washington. 'I don't know if this story is going in *Music* or *Show Business*,' he said.

'It should go in *National Affairs*,' said the CBS man.

Sullivan was talking about the Beatles. 'I remember the first time I saw them. I was at London Airport and there were mobs. There must have been 50,000 girls there and I later found out they had prevented Lord Home and Queen Elizabeth from taking off. I said to Mrs Sullivan, "Here is something". It was just like years ago when I was travelling in the South and I used to hear the name of Presley at fairs. Of course, he was all wriggling and sex. These boys are good musicians. When I finally saw them play in England, and the reaction, I said to Mrs Sullivan, "These boys have something".'

The *Time* man asked the press aide whether it was true that the Beatles had been invited to the White House.

'I understand the young girl is a big fan,' said the CBS man, 'but the Secret Service won't let her go to the Coliseum. I'm going to try and set up a performance at home.'

An hour before the Ed Sullivan programme was to begin, an instrumental trio wandered up and down the aisles serenading the largely teenage audience with soothing music. The fact that the only way back stage was through the men's room somewhat encouraged the girls to stay in their seats.

The troupe of boys from *Oliver* who were also to appear on the show arrived at the theatre. Someone asked them if they were Beatles.

'No,' replied a five-year-old with a Beatle cut and the broadest New York accent, 'we're roaches.'

Upstairs, the Beatles are having their pictures taken with Sullivan. A CBS press man is waving a pair of shears and a comb. 'C'mon, fellas,' he is saying, 'it's just a gimmick photo.'

Just before the programme is to begin, columnist Earl Wilson meets Sullivan backstage.

Wilson: 'Is it true, Ed? Are you going to wear it?'

Sullivan: 'I've already worn it.'

Wilson: 'How did you look?'

Sullivan: 'It's a wig like any other. By the way, your hair looks great.'

The next day the photograph with Wilson's column shows him wearing a bald wig.

The Beatles' recording manager, George Martin, is in the audience. He plans to record their concert at Carnegie Hall. Someone asks him why, since all the songs have been recorded before.

'I don't know,' he says. 'It's just a bit of history, I guess.'

Sullivan is on stage doing a warm-up. 'Listen, kids,' he says, 'there are other talented performers on this show,' (groans) 'so clap for them too.' (Perfunctory clapping.) 'We'll be going on in eight minutes.' (Groans.)

He walks off stage and reappears in a Beatle wig, and, to show the spirit of history that pervades, thanks Randy Parr for the wig. Miss Parr, it turns out, has persuaded her father to end his long feud with Sullivan in order to obtain a ticket for her to see the show.

The programme opens with an announcement of a congratulatory telegram from Elvis Presley and his manager Colonel Parker. Elvis says he is reciprocating the Beatles' telegram when he visited England in 1962, a visit unknown to all but Elvis. When the boys come on stage (screams), their names are superimposed on the screen. Under John's it reads, 'Sorry, girls, he's married'. In 'She Loves You' the screams for George and Paul's head-shaking are a split second late, but this, after all, is the first time they've been seen and the girls need time to coordinate their screams.

Backstage, Maureen Cleave wants to go up to their dressing-room but Sommerville tells her, 'My dear, they're changing their trousers.'

The door opens, and trumpeter Dizzy Gillespie walks in. 'What a mob!' he says as he is introduced to Sommerville by Alfred Aronowitz of the *Saturday Evening Post*.

'How do you do,' says Sommerville.

'Can I see 'em, man?' asks Gillespie.

Sommerville hesitates, and Aronowitz asks, 'Do you know who this is?'

'I've heard the name,' says Sommerville.

Just then George walks over. 'How do you do,' he says to Gillespie, and to Sommerville, 'I've lost me shoe.'

'I haven't come to hear you, man,' says Gillespie, 'I just want to get a good look at you.' He then asks George for his autograph and after receiving it tells him that he's 'going to sell it for two Count Basie records'.

During this exchange, Carol James, a Washington disc jockey, who had been the first to play a Beatle record in America, takes out a portable tape-recorder and begins to record the conversation. A CBS guard comes over, says that tape-recorders are forbidden in the studio, and throws James out.

As soon as James has been ejected George takes the ear plug from his transistor radio, holds it to Gillespie's mouth, and begins his own interview.

'Are you interested in Anglo-American relations?' he asks.

'Yes,' says Dizzy. 'I've got quite a few.'

The other three Beatles came downstairs with transistor radios, bearing the words Pepsi-Cola on them, plugged into their ears. They raced back to the Plaza, and, as they entered the door, a young man said to his date, 'They'll never believe it, never . . . We were so close.'

In one room of their suite George was assisting disc jockey Murray the K to broadcast his programme on Station WINS. The rest of the Beatles were listening to disc jockey B. Mitchell Reid on station WMCA. When he played 'I Want to Hold Your Hand' and, said 'A lot of people want to hold their noses,' they turned the radio off and returned to the other room. Murray the K told them that a group called 'Bonnie and her Butterflies' had been formed. 'She was going to be a Beatlette,' he said, 'but she thought of this butterfly gimmick, and her agent said, "Okay, now just fly, baby, fly".'

After the recording they went out for dinner to the Playboy Club. Asked his opinion of the Bunnies Paul said 'I think the Bunnies are even more lovable than we are.' Asked his opinion of the Playboy Club, he replied, 'No comment; the Playboy Club and I are just good friends.'

From the Playboy Club they went to the Peppermint Lounge, where they mistakenly thought the Twist was still being performed. In honour of their appearance the orchestra did play the appropriate music and Ringo twisted. The highlight of the evening, however, was when a group called the 'Seven Fabulous Epics featuring the Four Younger Brothers alias the American Beatles' took the stage. They had been doing a bewigged Beatle imitation for several weeks and performed the entire Beatle repertoire. 'It really wasn't much like us,' said Ringo afterwards, 'the music was too good.'

The next morning they stayed in the suite and over breakfast read the reviews of the Ed Sullivan show. The *Herald-Tribune* said that they were '75 per cent publicity, 20 per cent haircut, and 5 per cent lilting lament', and 'a magic act that owed less to Britain than to Barnum'. George said, 'The *Herald-Tribune* is fucking soft, talking about Barnum.'

The *Daily News* said:

Not even Elvis Presley ever incited such laughable lunacy among the screaming generation. The Presleyan gyrations and caterwauling, in fact, were but luke-warm dandelion tea compared to the 100-proof elixir served by the Beatles.

'The *Daily News*,' said John, 'knew what it was talking about.'

The *New York Times* assigned both its television and its music critic to cover the show. The television man, Jack Gould, wrote:

Televised Beatlemania appeared to be a fine mass placebo, and thanks undoubtedly are due to Britain for a recess in winter's routine. Last night's sedate anticlimax speaks well for continuing British– American understanding. The British always were much more strict with children.

The music critic wrote that 'The Beatles are directly in the mainstream of Western tradition. Their harmony is unmistakably diatonic.' Referring to the Fourth Leader in *The Times* he wrote: 'A learned British colleague has described it as pandiatonic but I disagree.' He said they 'have a tendency to build phrases around unresolved leading tones. This precipitates the ear into a false modal frame that temporarily turns the fifth of the scale into the tonic, momentarily suggesting the mixolydian mode. But everything always ends as plain diatonic all the same.'

In the afternoon, Harriet Van Horne, writing in the *World Telegram,* said the Beatles reminded her of her two favourite Saxon kings, Harold Blue Tooth and Ethelred the Unready.

The reviews were only one proof of the fact that, in the world of television at least, a common language is of very little use. On the same page as *The Times*'s reviews a programme was announced that would deal with Britain's new class structures. It went on to say: 'The documentary will include scenes from a fox hunt, a dinner party, and a shop where gentlemen are fitted for bowlers.'

The *Herald-Tribune*'s front-page story said: 'The Beatles apparently could not carry a tune across the Atlantic but were saved by the belles in the audience.' Their headline was that most puzzling of English phrases 'Beatles Bomb on TV'.

While the Beatles were still in their suite a notice went out on the teletypes in newspaper offices in New York. 'To the City Editor', it read. 'Information: The Beatles are now visiting the Museum of Natural History, 79th Street and Central Park West. Reporters and photographers are requested to go to the Museum's public relations office.' Twenty-seven minutes later the teletypes announced that 'the report of the Beatles visit proved to be a hoax.' The rumour had started when a young man told a museum guard he was a Beatle and was waiting for the other three. He said he had trimmed his hair when the publicity became too great.

The Beatles were to meet the press. Brown Megs, a Capitol Records executive, had spent several weeks compiling a huge press list. 'Sure I'm knocked out,' he told reporters, 'but Beatles only come once in a decade, if that.'

In the Plaza's Baroque Room the Beatles sat at a long table facing hundreds of reporters who sat on spindly-legged gilt chairs. They would raise their hands, be recognized by Sommerville, and ask questions. The answers they received led a writer on an afternoon paper to say, 'Obviously these kids don't care a fig about projecting any sort of proper image.'

'Which is a bigger threat to your careers – the H-bomb or dandruff?'

Ringo: 'The H-bomb – we've already got dandruff.'

'Do you have a leading lady for your film?'

'We're trying to get the Queen. She sells,' says George.

'When do you rehearse?'

'We don't,' says John.

'Yeah, of course we do,' says Paul.

'Paul does, we don't,' says John.

'You've been invited to a masked ball at the British Embassy. What are you going as?'

'Nobody told us,' says Paul, and then asks Sommerville, 'Is it true?'

Between press conferences they spent a few minutes posing for pictures with Dr Joyce Brothers. Dr Brothers, a well-known television psychologist, had come to the Plaza to 'psyche out the Beatles'. Her analysis ran the next day under a picture of Dr Brothers without her shoes having her pulse taken by Ringo. In addition to the 'psycheing out', Dr Brothers also provided some interesting coleopteran information:

Now that you've seen them, you're probably wondering why your children love them.

I mean the Beatles, of course.

Here's my theory:

Teenagers, as we know, feel themselves in revolt against adult society. This is perfectly normal and natural, and is part of the process by which young people 'find' themselves.

In fact, the only spots in the world where the adolescents don't 'ape' are in certain changeless primitive cultures where young men and women are expected to step into exactly the same roles their parents filled for thousands of years.

Adolescent rebellion appears to be an unavoidable trauma in any country which allows social change, individualism, and free choice of life style.

And what a trauma!

Naturally enough, it is difficult for parents to take it on the chin when the same child who so recently cried pathetically, if they dared venture to a neighbourhood movie without him, coldly announces that everything they have ever done or thought is 'for the birds'.

Most parents fight back.

They advise their teenagers that his or her behaviour is noisy, shiftless, vulgar, and no good, and that unless he reforms he will never amount to a hill of beans.

I recently heard a distinguished psychiatrist comment that even on an analyst's couch few adults can accurately recall the intense and violent emotions they experienced during adolescence.

It is such an unhappy period in many ways, that having outgrown it we gratefully block it out.

We honestly cannot believe that we ourselves were ever that unreasonable, sloppy, and goonish. And so, from generation to generation the war wages on.

The Beatles are a marvellous symbol to adolescents of their rebellion against adult society.

Not only do they 'get away' with being loud, vulgar, ridiculous, with gorging sweets and generally committing all the social crimes parents wring their hands at, these Beatles are actually rewarded for their behaviour.

They are rewarded handsomely. To the tune, it has been reported, of $100,000 a week.

Their Oliver haircuts and too-short jackets add to their mystique in a fanciful and original way.

Oliver Twist, you will recall, was an orphan. By embracing a quartet of orphans as heroes, our teenagers achieve two unconscious goals.

They symbolically 'kill off' the older generation.

They show how neglected and misunderstood they believe themselves to be.

Furthermore, consider the perfect significance of the very name 'Beatle', which, while it may be spelled differently, suggests certain small crawling creatures.

Beetles, like adolescents, might look unappetizing and inconsequential to a majority of humans, but naturalists have long considered them 'the most successful order of animals on earth'.

These insect pests show amazing tenacity, adaptability, and survival value, and number a staggering 250,000 species, as compared to a modest total of 36,000 for all vertebrates, including fish, reptiles, birds, and mammals.

Naturalists predict that beetles will survive long after man has passed from this planet, and, similarly, our teenagers expect to have the last word (which they will get).

The Beatles display a few mannerisms which almost seem a shade on the feminine side, such as the tossing of their long manes of hair.

These are exactly the mannerisms which very young female fans (in the 10- to 14-year-old age group) appear to go wildest over.

No doubt many of their mothers have wondered why. Girls in very early adolescence still in truth find 'soft' or 'girlish' characteristics more attractive than rigidly masculine ones.

They get crushes on their female school teachers, and on slightly older girls.

The male movie stars they most admire are apt to be the 'pretty boys' their big sisters would dismiss as kid stuff.

I think the explanation may be that these very young 'women' are still a little frightened of the idea of sex. Therefore, they feel safer worshipping idols who don't seem too masculine, or too much the he-man.

The Beatles describe themselves as 'unsexy' in relationship to girls. Ringo wears an abundance of flashing jewellery on wrists and fingers.

The point is that none of the Beatles is an obvious he-man symbol. No entertainer who ever clicks with the youngest teens ever will be.

As one psychiatrist put it:

'The little girls would be afraid to swoon in the presence of a Humphrey Bogart type. Who knows what he might do?

'With Beatles, they can let themselves go.'

One final observation about teenagers: young persons wish to be unlike adults, but like other teens. The best way to succeed with them is to seem offensive to adults, and to catch the eye of the vogue-setting teen leaders.

This, the Beatles have done.

The questioning went on through the afternoon and was followed by the reception in the Baroque Room. Although it was by invitation, the place was packed. At one point the beautiful wife of a New York department store owner cornered Paul and said invitingly, 'Gentlemen, gentlemen, gentlemen, don't you ever need a lady?' She ended up asking him what size shirt he wore.

When the president of Capitol Records, Alan Livingston, presented the Beatles with two gold discs for selling more than a million copies of their records, Epstein stood on the side with a look of *hauteur*. Several feet away, a Capitol official, observing the scene, remarked, 'Before Epstein came here he had ice-water in his veins. Now it's turned to vinegar.'

The Beatles were scheduled to fly to Washington the next day. It started to snow that night and they decided to go by train. Sommerville spent several hours on the telephone, trying to reserve a private car. The Beatles spent the evening in their suite, watching themselves on television, and reading their press cuttings.

Ann Arbor, Michigan (UPI). *Evangelist Billy Graham today placed himself in the camp of millions of American fathers. He doesn't dig the Beatles.*

Graham said that he broke his rule yesterday and watched television on the Sabbath – just to see the British quartet.

'I'm afraid I'm on a different wavelength than the Beatles,' he said. Mr Graham has three teenage daughters. He said he wanted to see the Beatles in an effort to understand teen life.

'They're just a passing phase,' he said. 'All are symptoms of uncertainty of the times and the confusion about us.'

The evangelist said he did not have much hope of ever fathoming Beatlemania.

'I hope when they get older they will get a haircut,' he said.

On television it was announced that in Las Vegas Elvis Presley had said, in welcoming the Beatles to America: 'If there's nothing but catfish in the market not many come to buy. If there are several kinds of fish it draws a bigger crowd, and that's good for show business.'

Before leaving the Plaza for Washington the next morning the Beatles learned that their appearance on the Ed Sullivan show had achieved the highest number of viewers ever recorded for an entertainment programme in New York.

Washington

'*Say, Home. About that Cyprus job. Afraid we're too busy right now protecting your Beatles.*'

Caption of a cartoon in the morning paper showing President Johnson talking on the telephone while outside the Beatles are being escorted by hundreds of armed tanks.

'*Sir Alec Douglas-Home has postponed his Washington visit by a day because of the Beatles' appearance there.*'

Ed Sullivan's column in the New York Daily News

'*I would like to see them very much but it's on a school night and I have a lot of homework.*'

Luci Baines Johnson in an official White House statement

The only private car that could be rented for the Beatles was an old Richmond, Fredericksburg, and Potomac sleeper called King George. It left New York's Pennsylvania Station in the middle of a snowstorm, and although the Beatles said that they had taken the train to 'see the country' they stayed in their compartments.

Occasionally, they would walk into the club car, where they would test their newly acquired American argot, mainly by saying 'That's beautiful, baby' to everything.

Their mentor, the disc jockey Murray the K, wearing stretch pants covered in zippered pockets, was talking to David English of the *Daily Express*. English mentioned that he had invited George to listen to Ella Fitzgerald at a night club in New York and that George had said she was an old fogey.

'You've got to be careful what you say to George,' said Murray the K, 'he takes everything very literally.'

He then walked over to Sommerville and told him that the BBC had asked him to do a programme for them.

'Do you think it's a good showcase?'

Sommerville told him it was. When he walked away he remarked, 'The boys like him now but they'll tire of him just like they do of everybody else.' He then started talking about memoirs in the *Sunday Express*, a topic he mentioned with increasing frequency.

Cynthia Lennon, wearing a brunette wig and dark glasses, walked through the train and started talking to a photographer from a fan magazine. He explained that he must use flash-bulbs for his work because the fans 'don't want to see all those arty pictures with freckles and pockmarks'.

When the train arrived at Washington's Union Station the Beatles were met by a crowd of journalists, many of whom wore Russian hats that lent a Tolstoyan air to the scene. There were only four teenagers, who carried a banner reading 'WWDC Welcomes the Beatles to Washington'. By the time the Beatles had walked the length of the platform, however, they were greeted by the kind of reception to which they were becoming accustomed. In the concourse nearly 3,000 teen-agers lined the barriers, breathed on the glass, hung through the bars, and climbed up the twenty-foot-tall platform gates.

'Thank God these kids can't vote,' said a journalist, as he was almost hauled aloft by the enthusiastic crowd.

From the station they were taken to a press conference at the Coliseum where they would be appearing that evening. A reporter asked them what they thought of President Johnson.

'What do you think of the President?' Ringo asked a stage hand who was adjusting the microphone.

'He's a great guy,' the man said.

'He's a great guy,' said Ringo.

In the bar of the National Press Club a correspondent was saying: 'Ringo certainly has a different style than Lyndon.' David English was entertaining his American colleagues by walking around with his hair over his eyes trying to explain the Beatles' attraction. The press aide to the British Embassy remarked to a correspondent that he hadn't been so busy since the visit of the Queen. 'First Burton,' he said, 'then the buses, and now the Beatles.'

The British atmosphere that pervaded Washington with the visit of the Beatles and the Prime Minister was sustained by the Art Theatre on K Street. Its marquee read: 'The Beatles in Color' and 'Christine Keeler Goes Nudist'.

The Washington Coliseum, where the Beatles were to give their first American concert, is usually used as a boxing ring or basketball court. Above the platform in the centre of the arena is a huge square score-box reading: 'Visitors – Home'.

Five hours before the show was scheduled to begin, the first customers were in their seats. At the entrance vendors hawked cotton candy, peanuts, Beatle wigs, and jelly-babies, as well as buttons reading 'I Love Beetles'. Two people tried to gain entrance with counterfeit photostats of tickets.

At eight o'clock, Carroll James, the disc jockey who had played the first Beatle record in America, introduced the impresario of the Coliseum. Then, in quick succession, came three American groups. Just before the interval a singer called Tommy Roe began to sing a song starting, 'I stood and watched, all night long; I stood and watched, all night long; I stood and watched, all night long; I stood and watched, all night long; I stood and CRIED all night long ...' He was drowned out by screams and a *sub rosa* cry of 'They're here!' 'They're in the dressing-room!'

After the interval a group of girls called the Chiffons began to sing. Directly in front of the ring-side platform stood their agent and their producer. They were approached by three teenage girls who asked whether they knew the Beatles. 'Yes, I do,' replied one of the men. Immediately, the girl broke into a frenzied scream. The two girls with her began screaming. In succession, the girls in the seats directly behind them started screaming as well. Within a moment, the entire audience of 8,092 was on its feet, screaming, shouting, whistling, and clapping.

As the noise reached a crescendo, the Beatles, escorted by twelve policemen, made their entrance. As they started to sing one of the policemen at the ring-side removed two ·38 calibre bullets from his belt and placed them in his ears. There is no rule against using flash-bulbs in the Coliseum, and from the top of the arena the atmosphere was like a thunderstorm with the screams and the flashing lights.

'No, I never heard them at all ...' sang Paul, and in Section 46, about a mile from the stage, they were listening to transistor radios and screaming.

By the platform in front of the television cameras, girls in pink stretch-pants are sobbing. 'Yeah, yeah, yeah,' sang George, and girls in boots, clenching their fists, shouted 'No, no, no.'

Between each number Sommerville runs on stage with tactical instructions on where to face. They sing 'Please, Please Me' and the shower of jelly-babies makes the ring-side seem like Omaha Beach.

Epstein, a polka-dotted foulard wrapped tightly about his neck, is standing aloofly by the entrance. People come over to speak with him but he doesn't reply. Next to him a young man in chino pants and tennis shoes is telling his companion, 'I think they're cool as hell.'

On stage they are singing, 'I Want to Hold Your Hand'. At its conclusion they drop their instruments and bolt up the aisle, surrounded by a flying wedge of policemen.

At the entrance a blond-haired boy asks 'Where did you go, mommy?' and is told, 'Oh, honey, I just couldn't bear it any more, I'm sorry.'

After a moment of stunned silence hundreds of girls begin to surge towards the platform. They begin to fight among each other for jelly-babies. A girl claws her way on stage to touch a guitar.

Backstage Ringo is delirious. 'Some of them even threw jelly-babies-in bags and they hurt like hailstones,' he is saying, 'but they could have ripped me apart and I couldn't have cared less. What an audience! I could have played for them all night!' Epstein walks into the room. They look up at him, their faces still dripping with sweat. 'I thought it was excellent, boys,' he says, and leaves the room.

On the way to the reception at the British Embassy George turned to Sommerville and asked, 'Who is this Ormsby Gore anyway?'

'Ormsby Gore,' replied Sommerville.

'Don't be soft,' said George. 'I know that, but is his name Ormsby or Gore?'

'It's Sir David Ormsby Gore.'

'Is he a lord?'

'No, he's a knight.'

'Was he gored when he was knighted?'

Before the reception the Beatles met the Ambassador and

Lady Ormsby Gore at the Embassy residence. When John is introduced to him Sir David says, 'Hello, John.'

'I'm not John,' says John, 'I'm Charlie. That's John,' and he points to George.

'Hello, John,' says the Ambassador, turning to George.

'I'm not John,' says George, 'I'm Frank. That's John,' and he points to Paul.

'Oh, dear!' says the Ambassador. 'I'll never get these names right. My wife is much better at remembering names.'

At the foot of the stairway in the rotunda of the British Embassy a group of women in evening dresses, and journalists in galoshes, were waiting for the Beatles to arrive.

'Well, after this,' says one matron, 'we can never again criticize the Americans for creating a sensation.'

'I know, my dear,' says another, 'that's why we're sending Caroline to school here. Heaven knows what's happening at home!'

Maureen Cleave walks over and says the Beatles thought the show at the Coliseum was 'the most fantastic thing they've ever seen'.

One of the women turns to her and asks, 'But in England don't they have to put plastic shields on the stage?'

At the entrance to the ballroom the Military Attaché, Major-General Roger St John, M.C., is trying on a Beatle wig for the benefit of a photographer from the *Daily Mirror*.

'But what does "Beatle" mean, anyway?' he is saying. 'Is it a euphemism for "roach"?'

A woman in the crowd looks at him and remarks, 'Oh dear! I hope the P.M. gets some of this press tomorrow!'

A man turns to Maureen Cleave. 'I'm from the President's space agency,' he says, 'and you have to admit this is pretty far out.' The announcer from CBS is singing 'Yeah, yeah, yeah' when the shout goes up, 'They're in the chancellory.'

They come down the stairs. A woman starts to scream. Paul walks with Sir David, John has Lady Ormsby Gore on his arm. Ringo wears a dark blue shirt. As they descend the stairs they gag for the photographs. At the bottom of the stairs John is grabbed by the man from CBS, who leads him over to a camera.

'Well, John,' he says, 'you are looking in the face of forty million people. How do you feel?'

'Do you really want to know?' says John.

Paul walks into the ballroom with the Ambassador and is approached by a slightly drunk woman, who puts her arms around him.

'Which one are you?' she asks.

'Roger,' says Paul.

'Roger what?'

'Roger McCluskey the fifth.'

Afterwards someone asks her what she thinks of the Beatles.

'Monstrous,' she replies.

After appearing on several television stations, posing for photos, and signing autographs, John walks into the rotunda for a drink. As he orders it an Embassy official is 'wondering' whether he can 'prevail upon our guests to participate in our rather small but not insignificant raffle'.

At that moment a young Embassy official approaches him and says 'Come along now! Come and do your stuff!' John glares at him. 'I'm not going back through that crowd,' he says. 'I want to finish my drink.'

'Oh, yes, you are,' the official says imperiously. 'Come on, come on.' John turns his back on the official, but is now approached by a young lady in a ballroom gown. 'Come along, now,' she says. Livid, John turns to Ringo and says, 'I'm getting out of here.' With a deadpan smile Ringo puts an arm on John's shoulder and answers calmly, 'Oh, come on, let's get it over with.'

While the Beatles draw the winning raffle tickets (the prizes are Beatle albums, and Ringo announces, 'If you don't like it, we can exchange it for a Frank Sinatra'), the same overzealous young aide is shoving and pushing several journalists. He is approached by the Embassy Press Secretary Frank Mitchell. 'Just because the system's broken down, Colin,' he says, 'you can't push journalists around who have paid to get in. She's the *Washington Star.*'

In the lobby of the rotunda, the photographer Robert Freeman is telling a young lady that he met the Beatles while studying 'the iconography of contemporary culture'. Her escort interrupts. 'Tell me,' he says. 'You seem to know them quite well. Doesn't all this have a bad psychological effect on them? I mean, doesn't it give them a trauma?'
'No,' replies Freeman, 'just other people.'

As the Beatles leave the ballroom a British débutante walks up to Ringo, removes a pair of nail scissors from her purse, and snips off a lock of his hair.

Just before they leave the Embassy, Lady Ormsby Gore tells them, 'Thank you so much for coming. I'm sorry about all that down there. It can't have been much fun for you.' Going out of the door, Ringo turns to the unsettled Ambassador and asks, 'And what do you do?'

When reports of what had happened were printed in the British press the Embassy issued a denial. When the Beatles insisted it was true, an M.P. posted a question to the Prime Minister regarding 'the disgraceful behaviour at the Embassy'.

The next morning they leave the hotel and make a brief stop to pose for photographs in front of the Capitol. On the train ride back to New York, while the camera team from Granada shoots film for their documentary, Ringo begins to slither around and under seats like an ape. Then John and George trade coats for no reason. Next, Ringo, with a dozen cameras around his neck pushes through the crowd, shouting, 'Excuse me! *Life* magazine! Exclusive! I am a camera!' Then George climbs up into the baggage rack above the seat and plays dead. Then Ringo scuttles through the car wearing a blond fur coat and a lady's white fur hat. Then George, wearing the porter's hat and white coat, comes in with a tray of empty coke tins. At the other end of the car Paul is flamboyantly taking pictures out of the window and shouting, 'God, how artistic! Railway lines!' The camera keeps filming; *Life, Newsweek,* and the *Saturday Evening Post* keep taking notes, and John occasionally looks up and mutters, 'Funny, very funny.'

Several hours later, Sir Alec Douglas-Home met President Johnson. The President remarked, 'I liked your advance party, but don't you feel they need haircuts?'

New York and Carnegie Hall

Manhattan

Dear Ringo,

I read in one of our newspapers that you are having some difficulty in finding a steady girl. Well, I wonder how you could possibly hope to, at this point in your career, when your schedule entails being whisked on to a plane, off a plane, into the limousines, away from screaming mob scenes, into a hotel, etc., etc., . . . all the madness of being 'on tour'! And why not? After all, the Beatles – like any other phenomenal stars – belong to their fans! Remember Caruso, Valentino, Elvis, Marilyn Monroe? It's sometimes unfortunate, but true!

Such an intimate endeavour as finding a girlfriend is out of the question – you're not Ringo Starr . . . or even Richard Starkey . . . now YOU ARE A BEATLE!

Ah! But you say that you are Ringo Starr . . . or Richard Starkey . . . or just plain (not literally!! by all means) YOU! Yes, all this is only too true! But right now, as the fans see it, you belong to them. The fact that you want to remain you is of no importance to them! Crazy, huh?

And if you do find a girl . . . some time between planes, hotels, shows, mobs and sleep . . . part of what she will ' see' in you is Beatle-ness. Don't knock it – it's charming. Really! But, of course, I agree with you – there's just got to be more! Being a Beatle should not be her only reason for ' digging' you! Not if you are ' soul-people', as I think.

But, remember, part of what makes you that person, by whatever name you wish to have people call you – or whatever name you refer to yourself – is also involved in a temporary form of ' insanity' – Beatle-mania. I believe it necessitates schizophrenia (not permanently) in each one of your foursome. But your girl exists in both the schizoid one and the real one – so she's got to have it for you in both, too! See? Other-wise, she can't keep up with you!

One more thing! All of the people that you are – Ringo, Richard, plus the others (perhaps, ' sans' names) deep inside you – must be real to her. And how in bloody hell is there a chance to pack the Beatle image in for the evening – or whatever – and be all those people, when you have to deal with all the headaches and hullabaloo of being famous??

Rough going, I'm afraid, but good luck anyway!

I guess my whole purpose in writing to you was to let you know that someone else feels what you're going through! It's too bad that there's so much red tape, too many mobs, hotels, aeroplanes, and all the rest!

I would have loved to meet you – to me you're a real person. I guess it's something about the way you look at people. Kinda with love.

> Sincerely,
> Clo

At the same time as the Beatles were leaving Washington, a crowd of girls began gathering on the Fifth Avenue side of the Plaza Hotel in New York. It was a school holiday and as the Beatles' train was speeding through Delaware nearly a thou-sand girls were milling about the Plaza.

Several times the crowd waving banners and autograph books crashed the restraining police barriers and mounted an attack on the hotel. At the doors, police reinforced by special guards stemmed the onslaught and drove the attackers back to the barriers. At one point police lines were broken, and the flag they had used to mark their command post at the fountain was snapped in two. During one assault a seventeen-year-old girl from Queens was knocked unconscious. Police carried her into the hotel. Her first words upon reviving were, 'Where are the Beatles?'

As the Beatles' train rolled through New Jersey, police with bull horns dispersed most of the crowd at the Plaza by telling them the Beatles were going directly to Carnegie Hall from Penn Station. Within minutes at least a thousand teenagers had gathered in the upper lobby of the railway station, and at least as many in the lower concourse.

When the train pulled in, the crowds swept aside the police barriers and, in a scene worthy of De Mille, deployed themselves in a frenzied search for track four and their idols. But it was not to be.

The Beatles' private car had been taken off the regular train and brought in on a separate track at the other end of the station. Railroad officials had planned to take them up a special elevator used for visiting royalty. There were fans waiting there also. Finally, the Beatles were taken from the lower level and spirited into a taxi in Seventh Avenue. Along the way they transferred to a limousine and an hour later arrived at the Plaza.

The car drew up to the 58th Street entrance and was engulfed by the crowd. Girls clambered on the roof, the hood, and the trunk, but the limousine, its horn blaring, continued to the Fifth Avenue entrance, where a thousand fans waited. A flying wedge of six policemen stood by the doors as the Beatles ran into the lobby.

In the Palm Court a violinist bravely kept playing as the Beatles rushed to the elevators. Six girls squeezed in with them. Two private guards were shoved aside by other girls trying to get into the elevator.

Surveying the scene, an Assistant Chief Police Inspector who was in charge of the operation said the fans 'appear to be deliberately trying to cause trouble'. He accused the Beatles' press agents of using buses to bring in the fans. When asked about this, Sommerville replied, 'I've never heard such utter twat in my life.'

THE BEATLES, HOTEL PLAZA, NEW YORK:
I SEE YOUR APPEARANCE AT CARNEGIE HALL IS ONLY
28 MINUTES – HOPE THIS IS A GAG BECAUSE HAVING
PAID $38.20 I'M GAGGING AT THE THOUGHT.

A half-hour before the Beatles' first performance at Carnegie Hall, the New York police said there were 5,000 persons milling about outside. This included about seventy-five young men from a local university, who marched up and down on the opposite pavement carrying signs reading 'Exterminate the Beatles'. Ten minutes before the show started, while the Beatles were being rushed down a freight elevator at the Plaza, a group of teenage girls rushed the pickets and destroyed the signs.

All 6,000 tickets (including 150 on stage at each show) had been bought within hours of going on sale. Just before the first show, Sidney Bernstein, one of the impresarios presenting the show, was explaining to reporters: 'It is a status symbol for the kids to be here, just as it's a status symbol for the 300 adults here tonight. I had to turn down David Niven, William Zeckendorf, and Shirley MacLainé for tickets, I just didn't have one left.'

Backstage, a group of policemen, guards, and ushers were preventing anyone from entering. They were meant to keep the fans out but they were also detaining the New York correspondents of the *Daily Express* and *Daily Mail*. The journalists finally got hold of Sommerville who threatened to 'cancel the show and take them back to London if all this doesn't stop immediately'. The correspondents were admitted. 'Moscow would treat us better', said Sommerville as he disappeared into the Beatles' dressing-room.

In the white and red plush hall whose opening concert Tchaikovsky came from Russia to conduct, there is a sign reading 'Beatles Forever', hanging from the top balcony. From the bottom is another, saying 'WE LOVE YOU'.

Bernstein comes on stage and asks the audience to preserve America's good image abroad by comporting themselves properly in the presence of the foreign press who are covering the concert. Then Murray the K comes on, tells several jokes, and warns the audience not to leave its seats or throw things. 'We have people especially to deal with things like that – but I'm sure you won't let it happen.'

Just before the Beatles arrive, the Briarwoods, a young folk-singing group, entertain. As they finish, the audience starts to cheer and they return for an encore. There is a sullen restlessness, but their second departure evokes a cheer that might have seemed an ovation under other circumstances.

During the Beatles' performance the stage seems to move because of the constant explosion of flash-bulbs. The red plush chairs prove particularly suitable for bouncing, and many of the audience take advantage of this fact. When Paul does his 'Little Richard' encore many of the girls are taken by surprise, but they quickly recovered and continue bouncing.

As they leave the theatre after the first show, a young girl turns to her two friends. 'God,' she says, 'it's the greatest catharsis I've ever had!'

At the same time a mink-coated matron turns to her companions and remarks, 'Well, anyway, I heard them but I don't know if that's good or not.'

Inside, thirty special policemen are searching the auditorium and find several girls hiding under seats and one under a blanket.

Outside, the audience for the second show begins to arrive. In the corner coffee shop the counterman is saying, 'So what's so different? All they do is scream just like all the others.' In his window is a sign reading, 'We love the Beatles', and next to it another reading, 'Why?'

During the second show several girls are given first aid beneath framed manuscripts of Ravel, Schubert, and Liszt. At one point a drunken woman tries to rush the stage, but she is restrained by police.

As the Beatles go on stage for the second time, an aide comes over and tells Bernstein that they kept the wife of New York's Governor Rockefeller waiting for half an hour outside their dressing-room during the interval. 'They just don't seem to care,' says the aide. Mrs Rockefeller had taken her children to the concert – the first time she had been seen with them in public since her divorce and remarriage.

'Apologize to Mrs Rockefeller,' says Bernstein wearily and sits down at the foot of a flight of stairs. 'I'm pooped.' He sips a bottle of cream soda and starts explaining how the Beatles arrived at Carnegie Hall.

'At college,' he begins, 'I was a political science major so for about ten or twelve years I've been reading the British papers. I kept reading about the Beatles and then when Sullivan had signed them I got Epstein's number through friends in England and called him up. I told him that I wanted to present them in a live appearance. He wasn't too excited. Then I suddenly got the idea – why not present them at Carnegie Hall? As soon as I said that, he immediately accepted over the phone. Now all I had to do was get Carnegie Hall.'

He takes a sip of soda and sighs. 'I went to the Carnegie Board,' he continues. 'Now, remember, they had turned down Elvis, and, the year before, I myself had tried to book Chubby Checker there. Anyway, they were cold to this too until I told them the Beatles' appearance would further "international understanding". Those were the magic words, "international understanding". They accepted.

'I decided only to place ads in the *New York Times* so we would attract a better kind of audience. At the time I was an agent with GAC so I got two financial partners, Hank Baron and Walter Heiman. Since the Beatles hadn't appeared yet in *Cashbox* we decided to ask the kids about them.

'Hank asked his son on a Friday to find out what his school was saying. By Monday the Beatles were twenty-three in *Cashbox* and number one in Westchester.

'I quit my job and became a full-time promoter. To further make Epstein happy I told him the other acts would all be serious folk music . . .'

Bernstein is interrupted by an aide. The Beatles have finished, and Mrs Rockefeller is being taken backstage where she would wait for the official limousine. Bernstein goes over to her and thanks her for coming. Mrs Rockefeller's daughter, Wendy, asks him whether he could get her a Beatle sweatshirt.

'Sure,' says Bernstein.

'Do you think you could get me three?' says Wendy.

Suddenly, one of the several dozen policemen milling about backstage shouts, 'Here they come!' A police sergeant runs over to Mrs Rockefeller and says, 'Watch out.'

'Quick!' says Mrs Rockefeller, grabbing her children and running into a doorway. 'Let's duck in here or we'll get trampled.'

A police captain rushes out. 'Is everything ready? Is everybody cleared? Okay, boys, here they come.' Suddenly, the Beatles shoot by, and are gone in a popping of flash-bulbs.

New York

Dear Beatles,

First of all, perhaps I should say that this is not a fan letter as such, in which I state that I love you all madly, etc. It is, rather, a brief note of thanks to you, as a group, from me, as an individual and as a self-appointed representative of my fellow-countrymen.

Perhaps you are not aware of this fact, but you are the first happy thing that has happened to us since the tragedy on November 22. You are the first spot of joy to come to a nation that is still very much in mourning, although the grief is now personal and unpublicized. It is for this reason that I extend my thanks and, somewhat arbitrarily, those of my fellow Americans, to you.

As I no doubt need not tell you, the responsibilities and demands of power are very great. Our nation, and to some degree, each individual American, has power; and each of us, perhaps even unconsciously, bears the burden of responsibility for the actions of our nation in the eyes of the world. For even a moment, if you let us show that we are not the cold, businesslike Yanks that so many believe us to be, then you will have done us a great service. You will have let us be uninhibitedly ourselves; you will have given us back, however briefly, our national identity.

Although I do not believe for a moment that this letter will arrive into your hands, I nevertheless feel the need to express my gratitude for the gift of joy; it has been a very rare commodity on this side of the Atlantic for the past few months.

Again, I thank you, and I wish you all the health and prosperity that your goodness deserves. May God be with you.

Sincerely yours,
Sharon Flood

When they flew to Miami the next day, their pilot wore a Beatle wig. American newspapers carried a UPI photo of an artist's conception of what they would look like without hair. The British press reported that for the first time in a year there was no Beatle record in the top ten. A columnist in the *Financial Times* asked: 'Can Beatlemania really be dying, even in the midst of some of the biggest publicity the group has ever had?' Meanwhile in Miami John and Paul took a few hours off to write a song called 'Can't Buy Me Love'. A week before the record was to be released in Britain and America, there were nearly three million advance orders – the largest advance sale in recording history.

In Miami they met Cassius Clay, who told them he was 'the greatest', but that they were 'beautiful'. *Time* magazine said they were 'really Teddy bears covered with Piltdown hair'.

The *Wall Street Journal* predicted that Americans would

spend fifty million dollars during the year on 'Beatle-associated merchandise' ranging from a Beatle motor scooter to a Beatlemobile for adults. Buttons saying 'I Hate the Beatles' appeared in Times Square souvenir shops, and Transact, the London-based organization that controls world licensing rights for Beatle products, spawned an American branch called Seltaeb to take care of business in the United States. Within several days there was a preliminary injunction in New York's Supreme Court concerning sweatshirts and another in Federal Court concerning one of the long-playing records.

Variety said the advent of the Beatles had 'shattered the steady, day-to-day domination of made-in-America music here and abroad. The British combo appears to have fundamentally shook up and globalized the music biz, and, from here on in, it's expected that a significant ratio of US best-sellers will be of foreign origin.' New records released while the Beatles were in Miami included 'My Boyfriend got a Beatle Haircut'; 'The Boy with the Beatle Haircut'; 'Beatle Bug' by the Bug Collectors; 'Beatle Crazy'; and 'The Beatle'. New groups were founded, including 'The Beatle-ettes', and 'The Bootles', whose trade mark was knee-high boots and whose first record was 'I'll Let You Hold My Hand'. Informing its readers of this group *Variety* headed its story 'Bootles Eying Beatles Boodle'.

Mention of the word 'Beatles' broke up a teenagers' concert being conducted by Leopold Stokowski. A television programme showed a picture of Mount Rushmore with John, Paul, George, and Ringo replacing Washington, Jefferson, Lincoln, and Roosevelt. *Cashbox*, the paper of the recording industry, said in an editorial that the Beatles were 'one of those rare American [*sic*] phenomena that come along only a handful of times in a generation'. *Newsweek* and the *Saturday Evening Post* ran the Beatles on their covers; *Newsweek*, showing only hair because George was ill and couldn't pose, was widely praised. The *SEP* cover, albeit its $100,000 worth of guarded equipment, showed George and Ringo scowling, and looked as if it was taken in five minutes. Only *Time* and the *New Yorker* used the word 'coleopteran' (the *New Yorker* being the only one to use it correctly).

Back in England they were called 'our best export' by the Prime Minister, and 'a useful contribution to the balance of payments'. They were invited to dinner by the Master of Brasenose College, Oxford, and praised by Prince Philip and Harold Wilson, who charged that 'the Tories are trying to make the Beatles their secret weapon'. John's book was published and *The Times Literary Supplement* said, 'It is worth the attention of anyone who fears for the impoverishment of the English language and the British imagination.' Passing James Bond and a biography of Edward VII, it became number one on the best-seller list. Ringo was elected a vice-president of Leeds University in preference to a former Lord Chief Justice, and the Queen expressed concern about the length of his hair. A group called the Icadas, which are large bugs that eat beetles, was formed, and four boys from Becket Grammar School, West Bridgford, Notts, sang 'A Me A Te', which is 'From Me To You' in schoolboy Latin. *Paris-Match* ran an article called '*Ces Beatles – est-ce vraiment un phénomène utile?*' that analysed why they were not successful in France.

The *New Statesman* printed an article by Paul Johnson called 'The Menace of Beatlism'. He wrote that: 'Bewildered by a rapidly changing society, excessively fearful of becoming out of date, our leaders are increasingly turning to young people as guides and mentors – or, to vary the metaphor, as geiger-counters to guide them against the perils of mental obsolescence.' During the following week the paper received nearly 250 letters about the article. The correspondents were three to one against Mr Johnson, and one reader suggested he try monkey glands.

A minister asked: 'In what aspect of the full life of the Kingdom of God can we find a place for the Beatles?' and a girl in Carlisle, when asked to name the present Pope, replied 'Paul', and when asked for the last one, 'John', and then volunteered that the next would be called 'Ringo'. An article in *New Society* by a former member of a Liverpool gang, now reading sociology, said that beat music was responsible for changing the structure of the Merseyside gangs and making the guitar their totem instead of the bicycle chain. The poet Stephen Spender said the Beatles' haircuts were 'antidotes to violence and adolescent sexuality because they are "compromise haircuts", as sexually indefinite as a mythical figure'. A woman in Derbyshire, looking at the tombs of her fifteenth-century forebears, said they had what looked like Beatle haircuts. A writer in the *Sunday Telegraph* said the group should break up because eventually they would all get married and 'the chances of four random women liking one another or even being able to get on with one another will be small indeed'. Their wax images were placed on permanent display at Madame Tussaud's.

The *Queen* ran a detailed analysis of the Beatles' finances, and the *Westminster Bank Review* ran a laudatory article entitled 'Twist 'n' Shout'. Derek Taylor left working on George's column to become Brian Epstein's personal assistant-cum-speechwriter, and an M.P. suggested introducing 'Beatle Bonds' to encourage teenagers to save their money. Jane Asher's brother Peter joined Gordon to record a Lennon and McCartney song called 'World Without Love', and the record rose to number one on the charts, displacing the Beatles. The *Sunday Express* reported that Dr Richard Asher, the father of Jane and Peter, had been missing from home for two months because of 'all the pressure', but the next day the *Daily Express* said he had returned. Borrowing a phrase from Ringo the Beatles' film was called *A Hard Day's Night*, and while the film was still shooting Princess Margaret and Lord Snowdon agreed to attend the première. *Panorama* devoted a programme to analysing Brian Epstein's career, and Foyle's honoured John with a lunch on the four hundredth anniversary of the birth of Shakespeare, receiving the largest request for tickets since they had honoured George Bernard Shaw.

A notice was placed in *The Times* Personal columns offering £2 for a signed first edition of John's book; Brian Epstein announced he was writing his memoirs – with the assistance of Derek Taylor; Brian Sommerville resigned his job and said in *The Times* that 'all suggestions' would be 'welcomed'.

A rumour that Paul had married Jane Asher swept America – *Life* magazine received hundreds of telephone calls asking whether it was true. A similar story circulated about Ringo and an eighteen-year-old apprentice hairdresser from Liverpool. Meanwhile, filming finished, the Beatles left for a month's holiday – their first in nearly a year. Paul and Ringo flew to the Virgin Islands. John and George, accompanied by Cynthia, flew to Hawaii, via Amsterdam, and Vancouver, British Columbia. They arrived in Honolulu in the middle of the night under assumed names. Within hours they were mobbed by fans. Shortly afterwards they left for Tahiti. As they flew off into the South Seas sunset George Harrison, the twenty-one-year-old lead guitarist and formerly an electrician's helper, pleaded to the world, 'Why don't you leave us alone?'

Practically every publication on earth, from the *Financial Times* to *Mad* comic has had a go at speculating on the reasons for all of this. The *Observer* said that 'Beatlemania has a long pedigree. Apart from compulsive dancing to drum-beats among Africans, young girls were known to have swooned when "the blades" swaggered through medieval Florence and squealed in eighteenth-century England as the redcoats marched by.' It also said that 'some experts find the subconscious significance of guitars intriguing. They fancy that their female symbolism is evident and point out that pre-Hellenic stone statuettes of women might well be mistaken for toy guitars.'

Newsweek informed its readers that 'women shrieked when Franz Liszt sat down at the piano; the German poet Heine, to account for the frenzy, turned to "magnetism, galvanism, and electricity . . . of histrionic epilepsy, of the phenomenon of tickling, of musical cantharides, and other unmentionable matters".'

The *New York Times* ran three stories on its front page analysing the Beatles, 'publicitywise', 'moneywise', and 'peoplewise'. In the latter article they quoted Dr Renée Fox, a sociologist, who said that the

most important answers to the Beatlemania question run much deeper than sex, status, and adolescent revolt. The wide range of the Beatles' appeal stems from their personification of many forms of duality that exist in our society. The Beatles constitute a treasure trove of such dualities.

For example, they are male and yet have many female characteristics, especially their floppy hair-dos. They also play the dual roles of adults and children. They appear to be good boys who nevertheless dress and pose as bad ones – London's Teddyboys.

Their fancy Edwardian clothes suggest a sort of sophistication that contrasts further with their homespun style of performance. Much has been made of their poor, lower-class backgrounds in northern England. Yet they are accepted by the upper crust, having attracted the auspicious attention of the Queen Mother, Princess Margaret, Mrs Nelson Rockefeller, and President Johnson.

Nor is this all. The Beatles, in their personal appearances, sing and play, but seldom can be heard above the shrieks of the audience, and so they almost play the role of mimes. In addition the four are both an audience for their own antics and for those of their cavorting, screaming audience, acting, as it were, a play within a play.

There is a Chaplinesque quality in their style. They convey the image of the absurd little man in an absurd, big world, bewildered but bemused by it at the same time. In America as in England the appeal of the Beatles is not confined to girls in their teens and younger, but spreads to boys and to many adults of both sexes. At least part of the attraction for adults lies in the Beatles' realistic attitudes towards their own success and their eventual eclipse.

In the Beatles people see four basically nice young boys who project some of the same contradictions that exist in many Americans, who are having a wonderful time at the acceptable expense of both themselves and their audience, who have expressed their gratitude for this fling and who have promised a graceful adjustment to the time when the party will be over.

The speculation goes on and on; the analyses are interminable. Probably the most authoritative, and certainly the most concise, answer was given months and months ago when the first of thousands asked, 'Why the Beatles? Why Beatlemania?' John Lennon, acting as spokesman for the group replied,

'Why not?'

Observations on the Eloi by the Time Traveller

FROM H. G. WELLS'S '*THE TIME MACHINE*'

In another moment we were standing face to face, I and this fragile thing out of futurity. He came straight up to me and laughed in my eyes. The absence from his bearing of any sign of fear struck me at once. Then he turned to the others who were following him and spoke to them in a strange and very sweet and liquid tongue.

. . . There was something in these pretty little people that inspired confidence – a graceful gentleness, a certain child-like ease. . . . And then, looking more nearly into their features, I saw some peculiarities in their Dresden-china type of prettiness. . . . The eyes were large and mild; and – this may seem egotism on my part – I fancied even then that there was a certain lack of the interest I might have expected in them.

As they made no effort to communicate with me, but simply stood around me smiling and speaking in soft, cooing notes to each other, I began the conversation. I pointed to the Time Machine and to myself. Then hesitating for a moment how to express time, I pointed to the sun. At once a quaintly pretty little figure in chequered purple and white followed my gesture, and then astonished me by imitating the sound of thunder.

For a moment I was staggered, though the import of his gesture was plain enough. The question had come into my mind abruptly: were these creatures fools? You may hardly understand how it took me. You see, I had always anticipated that the people of the year Eight Hundred and Two Thousand odd would be incredibly in front of us in knowledge, art, everything. Then one of them suddenly asked me a question that showed him to be on the intellectual level of one of our five-year-old children – asked me, in fact, if I had come from the sun in a thunderstorm! It let loose the judgement I had suspended upon their clothes, their frail light limbs, and fragile features. A flow of disappointment rushed across my mind. For a moment I felt I had built the Time Machine in vain.

I nodded, pointed to the sun, and gave them such a vivid rendering of a thunderclap as startled them. They all withdrew a pace or two and bowed. Then came one laughing towards me, carrying a chain of flowers altogether new to me, and put it about my neck. The idea was received with melodious applause; and presently they were all running to and fro for flowers, and laughingly flinging them on me until I was almost smothered with blossom. You who have never seen the like can scarcely imagine what delicate and wonderful flowers countless years of cultivation had created. Then someone suggested that their plaything should be exhibited in the nearest building, and so I was led past the sphinx of white marble, which seemed to watch me all the while with a smile at my astonishment, towards a vast grey edifice of fretted stone. As I went with them the memory of my confident anticipations of a profoundly grave and intellectual posterity came, with irresistible merriment, to my mind.

I began a series of interrogative sounds and gestures. I had some considerable difficulty in conveying my meaning. At first my efforts met with a stare of surprise or inextinguishable laughter, but presently a fair-haired little creature seemed to grasp my intention and repeated a name. They had to chatter and explain the business at great length to each other, and my first attempts to make the exquisite little sounds of their language caused an immense amount of amusement. However, I felt like a schoolmaster amidst children, and persisted, and presently I had a score of noun substantives at least at my command; and then I got to demonstrative pronouns, and even the verb 'to eat'. But it was slow work, and the little people soon tired and wanted to get away from my interrogations, so I determined, rather of necessity, to let them give their lessons in little doses when they felt inclined.

Seeing the ease and security in which these people were living, I felt that the close resemblance of the sexes was, after all, what one would suspect; for the strength of a man and the softness of a woman, the institution of the family, and the differentation of occupations are mere militant necessities of an age of physical force.

A queer thing I soon discovered about my little hosts, and that was their lack of interest. They would come to me with eager cries of astonishment, like children, but like children they would soon stop examining me and wander away after some other toy.

Acknowledgements

For photographs in this book we are indebted to:

Leslie Bryce, Beat Publications; *Daily Express*; Robert Freeman; *Hatami/Paris*; Dezo Hoffmann; *Honey* magazine; *Mirrorpic*; Norman Parkinson; Rex Features; United Press International.

Most of the quotations on pages 13–15 are drawn from exclusive interviews with the Beatles by Miss Maureen Cleave and were published by the *Evening Standard* in a series of articles by Miss Cleave under the title 'The Year of the Beatles' during October 1963. The author is indebted to the *Evening Standard* and to Miss Cleave for permission to re-publish these remarks.

The extract from H. G. Wells's *The Time Machine* is reprinted by permission of the Executors of H. G. Wells, and Messrs William Heinemann Ltd.